A Lost God in a Lost World

From deception to deliverance;
a plea for authentic Christianity

Melvin Tinker

EP BOOKS
1st Floor Venture House, 6 Silver Court, Watchmead,
Welwyn Garden City, UK, AL7 1TS

web: http://www.epbooks.org

e-mail: sales@epbooks.org

EP Books are distributed in the USA by:
JPL Distribution
3741 Linden Avenue Southeast
Grand Rapids, MI 49548
E-mail: orders@jpldistribution.com
Tel: 877.683.6935

British Library Cataloguing in Publication Data available

ISBN 978-1-78397-122-0

Melvin Tinker's analysis is characteristically clear, punchy, perceptive, and penetrating. *A Lost God in a Lost World* is another magnificent example of wide-ranging and carefully applied biblical exposition from one of England's leading pastor-theologians.

Benjamin Dean, Dean of Postgraduate Studies, Lecturer in Systematic Theology, George Whitefield College, Cape Town, South Africa

A Lost God in a Lost World is an invitation to turn from gods of our own imagination to look at the real God. It's an invitation to a bigger view of the human problem and a bigger view of God. It's a transforming vision. In a restless, rootless world, here is a firm foundation. For a church drifting to the margins of the culture, here is a way forward—not through a new technique or methodology, but through a renewed understanding of the triune God. *A Lost God in a Lost World* delivers cultural reflection and biblical insight in a highly accessible manner.

Tim Chester, pastor of Grace Church, Boroughbridge, and tutor with the Acts 29 Oak Hill Academy

Addressing the confusion of modern life, Melvin Tinker offers a sure guide to both the crisis of our time and the way to confront and overcome it. His approach is direct, to the point and compelling in the force of its logic. This is a book for both individual and group study and will challenge its readers with both the tragedy of human life and the solution provided by God in Jesus Christ.

Gerald Bray, Research Professor of Divinity, Beeson Divinity School, Samford University

That the church in the West is at crisis-point few would deny. The question is: what can be done? Some suggest better management and structuring; others advocate more shift with the culture. Melvin Tinker plumbs deeper, arguing for a Christian integrity based on glorious but all-too-neglected core truths. With winning clarity, this book expounds those humanising truths which can reform and refresh the church. Bracing and fortifying, this is a tonic for today.

Dr Michael Reeves, Director of Union and Senior Lecturer, Wales Evangelical School of Theology, Bridgend

Melvin Tinker's book powerfully addresses the heart of an issue that lies behind many of the ills of Christian life in this age: reducing God to the measure of our own minds, and trying to bend his will to meet our own desires. With each chapter focusing on a different passage of Scripture and highlighting a different aspect of God's glorious character and work, he refreshes us by showing our great need for God in his greatness and glory.

Dr Tim Ward, Associate Director of the Proclamation Trust's Cornhill Training Course

For Mark and Becky Lanier
The Hull Mission Team
And all the members of the
Lanier Biblical Literacy Class, Houston, Texas.

Contents

Foreword

Today, we are in the midst of a massive, breathtaking transformation in world Christianity. What is changing is where it lives. Fifty years ago, residentially speaking, it was overwhelmingly Western. This is no longer the case. Today, the majority of those who see themselves as Christian are found in the global South and many of them, of course, are evangelical. In fact, the numerical 'center' of Christian faith is somewhere not far from Timbuktu in Mali, West Africa! This center is the place from which equal numbers of Christians are to be found in all directions. Once this center was in Europe. Now it is not. That is the change that has taken place.

This transition from North to South, and European to non-European, means many things. It means, of course, that the face of world Christianity has changed. It is now younger, less educated, less White, and less affluent than it was fifty years ago. But what is much more important than this is to ask why Christian faith, at least when judged by numbers and regular church attendance, is stagnating in the West while it is exploding in the global South.

And while Christian faith is stagnating in the West, it is also being brushed off as irrelevant by more and more people in these Western countries. This, of course, happened first in Europe. Behind this development were many others but the change came into public view unmistakably in the rampant secularism of the 1960s and 1970s. And this happened not just in Europe. The same thing was also going on in places like Canada, Australia, and New Zealand. Indeed, this seemed to be the calling card that the modernized world was leaving behind everywhere.

The United States, though, was initially resistant to this development. It is true that in the 1970s a vigorous literature did spring up around 'secular-humanism,' some lauding it and others bemoaning it. However, America was, at the same time, significantly religious. But then, remarkably, in both Europe and America, people began to turn spiritual. Some people who are spiritual are, at the same time, religious. Indeed, they are spiritual because they are religious. What changed was the number of people who say they are spiritual but insist that they are *not* religious. They do not belong to any organized religious group nor do they believe any religious doctrine. These spiritualities, in fact, have become especially unfriendly to historic Christian faith. So, the faith that was initially just brushed off as being merely irrelevant in Western countries is now more often resented and even aggressively opposed.

Christians in Europe have had some time to get used to their marginal existence but Americans are more perplexed by it. This was the subject explored in James Hunter's 2010 book, *To Change the World: The Irony, Tragedy, & Possibility of Christianity in the Late Modern World.* He criticizes the bloated ambitions and language of Christians who, in recent years, have sought to 'impact' culture, to 'transform it,' and to 'take back the country.' Hunter argues that all of this has been misguided. It has misfired and put Christians in an even more tenuous position. Instead, he calls for a more modest Christian 'presence,' through a 'faithful presence,' in society.

This is a needed corrective. Christians have sometimes been naïve about the complexity and the difficulty of bringing about change in highly modernized societies. They have not always understood how cultural networks work and how cultural elites exercise their power. At the same time, can we be content with a faith that is privately engaging but, at the same time, disengaging from the world around it?

In the early fifth century, barbarian hordes had come south out of Europe and moved toward the heart of the Roman empire. Then the unthinkable happened. Under the Visigoth leader, Alaric, barbarians entered Rome itself in 410 AD. They simply walked into the city and sacked it. They really did not have to conquer it. They were uncontested. Rome had already collapsed from within. It fell victim to its own moral corruption, its lost vision, and its own inertia. For decades prior to this moment it had also failed to cope with the massive flood of immigrants who made their way into the empire. As the empire tottered, it relied more and more on a stifling bureaucracy to compensate for the effects of its own internal decay and emptiness. This only succeeded in suffocating the city and the empire. Then, after the dreadful moment when startled Roman citizens awoke to the sight of Visigoths on their streets, the lights in the empire slowly went out. The Roman world died and the Dark Ages began.

This unexpected event provoked two very different responses. The one came from Augustine and the other from monasticism. One was the way of engagement, the other of retreat.

From Augustine came his *The City of God*. It was most immediately an answer to the way pagan Romans were thinking about the fall of Rome. They imagined that this was an act of revenge by the gods because so many Romans had turned to Christian faith. But Augustine's work was also much more than an answer to this false charge. It was the first sustained Christian reflection on divine providence. It offered a rich and profound philosophy of history. It gave an explanation of the interconnections between the Earthly City—human life in its fallenness and with all of its false deities—and the City of God (which is the kingdom of God). As difficult and even as perilous as it was, Augustine engaged his world. Indeed, he outthought his opponents. And he lifted up Christian eyes to see the greatness, sovereignty, power, and grace of God.

The other response was quite different. It involved a tactical retreat. While the empire was falling apart and the crude ways and customs of the occupying barbarians were becoming entrenched, Christian faith withdrew. It found a special place to live in the monasteries. There its learning was indeed preserved as Thomas Cahill has argued in his *How the Irish Saved Civilization*. But there, too, Christian faith lived in seclusion from the world around it.

Today in the West, this response to the world is having some resonance. Some Christians are now considering the 'Benedict Option.' That is, they are thinking that Western cultures are now so corrupt and so inhospitable to Christian faith that a tactical retreat is in order, one similar to what happened following the destruction of Rome. But while this retreat might lead to more Christian comfort it does not lead to more Christian witness or to more Christian faithfulness. Ours, in fact, is a time calling in a loud voice for Augustine, not for more cloisters.

All of our modern Christian dilemmas come back to a single place. That place is the greatness, goodness, and grace of God. Indeed, this has been the perennial issue among God's people in all ages. Are they remembering who God is or are they forgetting him?

The truth is that whenever Christian faith turns worldly and becomes powerless, as it so often has in the West today, it is because it has lost sight of him. The present 'age' has eclipsed the 'age to come,' the Earthly City obscures the City of God, because the God whose age and City it is has disappeared from our sight. We are no longer hearing the music from this other world. The impulse to retreat, even to hide, is only strong when the power of God seems less real to us than the power of the present moment. If our vision of God is clouded, or our knowledge of him is deformed, living in a hostile cultural climate becomes an unequal contest.

So I welcome this fine book. I appreciate the fact that Melvin Tinker has gone to the heart of the matter, to the very center of our faith. Evangelical faith is never going to be renewed by better marketing techniques, or more cultural accommodations, slicker presentations, or better business acumen. It will be renewed only when our knowledge of God is deepened, our walk with him becomes more genuine, our faith more authentic, and our churches more biblical. This is exactly what this book calls for. It sets up the doctrinal structure of Christian faith and lays out with great clarity the truth that these doctrines declare. And he shows that as pressing, and sometimes as novel as our challenges seem to be today, they are actually the recurring challenges that God's people have faced in every generation. Here, though, he deals with those challenges from within the biblical period and lays out the biblical answers. If we would but listen we might be quite surprised at the results! We would see the gospel making inroads into our Western world, the Church finding new life, and Christians living with greater confidence and more hope. May it indeed be so!

Dr David Wells
Distinguished Senior Research Professor
Gordon-Conwell Theological Seminary

Preface

'Luke-warm Christianity' is not what I once thought it was. The risen and ascended Christ's warning to the self-satisfied church of Laodicea in Revelation chapter 3 seemed clear enough; their deeds were 'neither hot nor cold', instead they were 'lukewarm'. Jesus said that he preferred them to be 'one or the other'. Therefore, to me Jesus was saying that a frigid, cold Christian congregation was better than one which was just tepid. The judgement Christ pronounced was shocking and severe, 'I am about to vomit you out of my mouth'. The moral of that, so I thought, was the need to be a 'hot' Christian, all out for the Lord.

But upon understanding a little more of the background to this passage, I discovered that the issue was not spiritual zeal as such, but spiritual *usefulness*. The reality behind the imagery Jesus was drawing upon was the plumbing system of this ancient city. In the Lycus valley where Laodicea was situated, there were two other New Testament towns; Colossae and Hierapolis. Colossae enjoyed water which was fresh and cold and therefore useful. Hierapolis, on the other hand, had water which was hot and medicinal, flowing from hot springs in which people bathed for their health. Its water was also useful. Laodicea, however, had to draw its water from miles away by stone pipes which left thick, carbonate deposits in the plumbing system, making the water disgusting to drink. In effect, the risen and ascended Lord Jesus was saying to this church: 'I wish that you were like the water of Colossae—cold and useful. Or like the water of Hierapolis— hot and useful, but you are neither. You have become like the water you drink—indigestible and so useless.'[1] This painted a different picture of nominal Christianity altogether! It meant that it was possible to be an active, apparently vibrant and seemingly 'successful' church, even having the name 'Evangelical', and still be ineffective in the sight of Christ and thus coming under his judgement.

This is Laodicean Christianity both past and present.

What is the problem?

The answer is given by the passage itself. The church was hardly distinct from its surrounding culture. The materialistic, self-sufficient, proud outlook of the town of Laodicea had been taken on by the church and given a Christian veneer. The real tragedy was that Christ had been left outside to knock on the church door and no one seemed to have noticed his absence; 'You say, 'I am rich; I have

---

1. D. A. Carson, 'Approaching the Bible', in *New Bible Commentary, 21st Century Edition* (InterVarsity Press, 1994), p. 15.

acquired wealth and do not need a thing.' (v 17); 'Here I am! I stand at the door and knock. If anyone hears my voice and opens the door, I will come in and eat with that person, and they with me.' (v 20). There is still hope—*if* the church listens and repents.

Laodicean nominalism is rife on both sides of the Atlantic. The danger is that the more 'successful' a church becomes in terms of its numbers, buildings and 'pulling power', the more prone it is to Laodiceanism.

All the indicators are in place that this is the case, as are the statistics which have been well rehearsed.

Amongst members of prominent mega-churches in the United States, Rodney Stark found:

Only 46% attend services weekly or more often

Only 46% tithe

Only 33% read the Bible daily[2]

The concern is what lies further down the road amongst the young.

A number of years ago the sociologist Christian Smith conducted a survey of hundreds of children in the United

---

2. Rodney Stark, *What Americans Really Believe* (Waco: Baylor University Press, 2008), p. 47.

States who were children of conservative Christian parents—those who went to 'bible teaching churches'. He discovered that in general American teens practiced what he dubbed 'Moralistic Therapeutic Deism'. This is a bland relativistic spirituality which emphasises doing good and feeling good and believing in a harmless, benevolent, one-size fits all God. This God doesn't interfere with how we live our lives, so long as we are sincere. Not surprisingly, one of the most notable findings was the absence of any connection between biblical thinking and day-to-day living. Smith writes, 'Quite often, teens said they did not think their religious faith affected their family relationships, they did not believe religion was relevant to the conduct of a dating relationship, they did not see that religion affected their life at school and so on.'[3]

In the United Kingdom the situation is hardly any better. A recent survey found that amongst self-designated Evangelicals in the age range of 16–24 years, only 38% read the Bible daily. This group is 'less likely to strongly agree that the Bible has supreme authority in guiding their beliefs, views and behaviour; are less likely to give money, and faith is less likely to be a key factor in their decision making'.[4]

Dr David Wells summarises the situation succinctly: 'We have turned to a God that we can use rather than to a God we must obey; we have turned to a God who will fulfil our needs

---

3. Christian Smith, Soul Searching: *The Religious and Spiritual Lives of American Teenagers* (New York: Oxford University Press, 2005) p. 140.

4. Evangelical Alliance, 21st Century Evangelicals—a Snapshot http://www.eauk.org/church/resources/snapshot/21st-century-evangelicals.cfm.

rather than the God before whom we must surrender our rights to ourselves. He is God for us, for our satisfaction—not because we have learned to think of him this way through Christ but because we have learned to think of him this way through the marketplace.'[5]

More recently, social critic, Dr Os Guinness has analysed the twin crises of the church and the West suggesting that we may be facing an 'Augustinian moment.'[6] It was when Roman/Christian civilization was on the verge of collapse that Augustine of Hippo wrote his *magnum opus*, *City of God*, with the timely reminder that there is an abiding City of which Christians are citizens that can never be shaken and we are to live out our lives in this world as members of the coming world. However, Guinness warns, 'The world to come will be shaped by whether the worldwide Christian church recovers its integrity and effectiveness and demonstrates a faith that can escape cultural captivity and prevail under the conditions of advanced modernity – or does not.'[7] The call is to seek under God a new Christian 'Renaissance'. He then lays down this challenge, 'that we trust in God and his gospel and move confidently into the world, living and working for a new Christian renaissance, and thus challenge the darkness with the hope of the Christian faith, believing in an outcome

---

5. David F. Wells, *God in the Wasteland* (Grand Rapids: Eerdmans, 1996), p. 114.

6. Os Guinness, *Renaissance: the Power of the Gospel However Dark the Times* (Downers Grove, IL: IVP, 2014).

7. Os Guinness, *Renaissance* p. 26.

that lies beyond the horizon of all we can see and accomplish today.'[8]

The modest aim of this book is to present those key truths about the lostness of man, the greatness of God and the glory of the future which will correct much wrong thinking and behaviour within the church and so enable the church to effectively confront the world by holding out the Gospel. This book has been written in order to enable Christians to trust 'the God who is there' and his gospel and so enable them to move confidently into the world.

The chapters are 'expositional' in nature, unashamedly so, as this, I believe, enables one to be most controlled by the Bible text itself and be rigorous in application. These are 'preached' truths, for, as J. I. Packer is so fond of saying, the Bible itself is 'God preaching'.

The title chosen may seem strange at first sight.

Christians may understand that we live in a lost world, but how can God be lost? Of course he can't be, not as we can get lost in a dark forest. But it is my conviction that what has been lost (or is in danger of being lost) in many churches (including those who would own the term 'evangelical') is a robust, fully orbed view of the Biblical God; a God who is wonderfully Trinitarian and who alone can act to free the church from its self-imposed cultural captivity.

---

8. Os Guinness, *Renaissance*, p. 28.

What is more, the biblical view of the 'lostness of the lost' has been lost. The recurrent problem of idolatry, the natural human condition of bondage to sin is either ignored or downplayed in our churches. The result is that God-dependent evangelism becomes replaced by presentations of the faith which are focused on felt needs rather than the deeper underlying need of liberation from sin.

A sole concern for the present can lead to short-term pragmatism and, if things don't work out as we would wish, to pessimism and cynicism. It is therefore vital that we have set before us a picture of the future new heaven and earth.

These are some of the major biblical themes this book seeks to address in the hope, that under God, we shall become more effective instruments of righteousness in his hand for the salvation of many and the glorification of his name.

I wish to express my deep and profound thanks to Mark Lanier and the wonderful staff of his impressive theological library in Houston, Texas, for the use of this marvellous resource. It is a genuine privilege to study in such an environment which not only has at hand many valuable books for reference, but provides such a godly atmosphere in which to work.

I would also like to express my gratitude to the staff and congregation of the church family which it is my privilege to serve—St John, Newland, Hull. I am grateful for their encouragements as they seek to be faithful to the God who speaks from his Word and in seeking to introduce others to this God in evangelism.

Last, but by no means least, I wish to thank my wife Heather who remains my best friend, critic and inspiration.

Soli Deo Gloria

Melvin Tinker
The Lanier Theological Library
Houston
Texas
2015

1

When God is Weightless

The Problem of Idolatry, Isaiah 44:9–23

One of the greatest hindrances to the flourishing of the Christian faith in the West is not unbelief but belief. It is not that Britain, for example, is full of unbelievers, those who are ardent atheists. The likes of Professor Richard Dawkins, Sam Harris and Stephen Fry are, in fact, few and far between. Rather the West is made up of many *believers*. How can this be so? To answer that question we need to ask a prior question: what are the marks of *any* believer?

There are three things: first, a believer *worships*. This is not just a matter of adoration and praise, but whatever a person gives themselves over to as the centre of their world, in short, what they live for. Secondly, the believer *serves* so that what is seen as the ultimate goal in life is what we give ourselves over to working for. Thirdly, a believer *proclaims* or to use a more contemporary term—*advertises*. Here there is the inner compulsion to tell other people about what drives and directs us in our day–to-day living. With the rise of social media the power to do this is unprecedented in the history of the human race.

When we take those three features of a 'believer'—someone who worships, serves and proclaims—it becomes pretty obvious that the West is made up of believers alright, but not Christian believers. It is composed of what the Bible calls idolaters, people who believe in things, maybe even in 'god', but usually one of their own making, other than the one true God of the Bible.[1] What is more, as we shall see, idolaters are to be found as much *within* the church as outside it.[2]

The pull towards idolatry has always been a constant problem for God's people. It is clearly there in Isaiah's day amongst Jews who with their mouths would recite daily their 'creed', the *Shema* of Deuteronomy 6:4-5, 'Hear, O Israel:

---

1. A notable example of an advocate of DIY religion is the singer Annie Lennox. On the CD sleeve of her collection of traditional Christmas carols, *A Christmas Cornucopia* she writes, 'While I don't personally subscribe to any specific religion, I do believe that the heart of all religious faith has to be rooted in love and compassion, otherwise it serves no purpose. For me the word 'Christ' represents the sacred and mysterious divinity in life ... which could just as easily be 'Buddha' or 'Allah'.

2. Carl Trueman suggests that in considering modern day idolatries, the Marxist concept of the *fetish* is a useful concept readily at hand, 'A fetish is something to which human beings ascribe a power it does not possess in and of itself.' 'The Banality of Evil', in *Minority Report—Unpopular thoughts on everything from ancient Christianity to Zen-Calvinism* (Mentor, Christian Focus, 2008) p. 83.

The Lord our God, the Lord is one. Love the Lord your God
with all your heart and with all your soul and with all your
strength', but who by their lives demonstrated that they
worshipped anything *but* the Lord their God alone.[3] Neither
is it insignificant that the apostle John writing to Christians in
his own day ends his first letter with the terse command 'Dear
children, keep yourselves free from idols' (1 John 5:21). From
the beginning of the Bible to its end, idolatry is seen as the
besetting sin of the human race. Indeed it defines sin because
sin is an attempt to dethrone God by putting ourselves or
something else in his place. It is the 'original sin'. Idolatry lies
at the heart of human rebellion. As one writer has recently
put it, 'In the Bible there is no more serious charge than that
of idolatry'.[4]

---

3. Daniel Block has extensively argued that the main purpose of the Shema is
to reinforce Israel's covenant allegiance to Yahweh alone and so can be rendered
accordingly as 'Our God is Yahweh, Yahweh alone'; 'The Shema should not
be taken out of context and interpreted as a great monotheistic confession.
Moses had made that point in 4:35, 39: "For Yahweh (alone) is God; there is
none beside(s) him." Nor is the issue in the broader context the nature of God
in general or his integrity in particular—though the nature and integrity of his
people is a very important concern. This is a cry of allegiance, an affirmation of
covenant commitment in response to the question, "Who is the God of Israel?"
The language of the Shema is "sloganesque" rather than prosaic: "Yahweh our
God! Yahweh alone!" or "Our God is Yahweh, Yahweh alone!" This was to be
the distinguishing mark of the Israelite people; they are those (and only those)
who claim Yahweh alone as their God.' Daniel I Block, 'How Many is God? An
investigation into the meaning of Deuteronomy 6:4-5' *JETS* 47/2 (June 2004)
pp.193–212.

4. Brian S Rosner, 'The Concept of Idolatry', *Themelios* (Vol. 24, No 3, 1999)
p. 21.

The implications of this present state of affairs is accurately assessed by the Christian thinker, Harry Blamires:

> Now accepting this as a Christian account of 'belief', what about the man who says, 'Oh yes I believe in God,' when his mental orientation, his overall purposes, and his conversational obsessions reveal that in fact he believes primarily and earnestly in the ladder of promotion, the achievement of the maximum number of personal comforts, and the promiscuous pursuit of the opposite sex? Surely he is guilty of a lie if he pretends that he believes in God, when he really believes in promotion, comfort and sex. Conversely, what about the man who says, 'No, I don't believe in any God,' when his mental orientation, his daily activity, and daily chatter reveal that he believes passionately and profoundly in money, cars, and gambling. Surely he too is guilty of lying. His gods are money, cars and gambling. To call one man a believer (theist) and the other an unbeliever (atheist) would be most misleading when one believes in promotion, comfort and sex, and the other believes in money, cars and gambling. For practical purposes they are both polytheists. In this sense, it is not atheism and not scepticism, but polytheism that is endemic in our day. The question that should be asked by the pollster on the doorstep is not "Do you believe in God?" but "Which God do you believe in?"[5]

The word frequently used in the Old Testament translated 'idol' (*aven*) at root means something which is 'empty' or 'weightless'. This stands in sharp contrast to the term

---

5. Harry Blamires, *Where do we stand? An Examination of the Christian's Position in the Modern World* (SPCK, 1980), p. 120.

which appears over and over again to describe God—
'glory' (*kabod*)—denoting something of immense weight,
overwhelming fullness. When we turn away in our hearts
from the one true God we engage in a cheap exchange,
swopping the one who is of infinite weight and worth for
something which is empty and worthless.[6]

This is precisely what is happening in our culture today.

We are in danger of having lost God. Not that God has been
lost as when we misplace a set of keys, but rather that the
truth about the real God is disappearing fast. What is more,
when God is lost from sight, we become lost too. A lost God
results in a lost world. In terms of purpose we never find
satisfaction, in terms of morality, we have no fixed points and
in terms of human life, it loses its unique value.

It is not difficult to cast around for examples of such losses
at every turn.

Take the sense of purpose and satisfaction. Through

---

6. 'The most commonly used Greek term for idol, *eidolon*, which occurs
almost 100 times in the LXX, lends itself to such polemic and is effectively a
term of derision. The established association of the word with insubstantiality
and falsehood provided the pejorative element in the description of an image ...
Disgust and contempt for idolatry is also communicated in several derogatory
terms used to describe idols. Idols are 'unclean things', a common designation
in Ezekiel, 'weak/worthless things', 'that which is insubstantial', and a 'vanity'
or 'emptiness'. The Israelites were not simply to avoid idolatry; the language of
prohibition could hardly be more emotive and urgent; they are to 'utterly detest
and abhor' the heathen gods (Deuteronomy 7:25f)' Rosner 'The Concept of
Idolatry', p. 22.

magazines, chat shows and general media frenzies, celebrities
are put forward as the beautiful people to be envied.
Popularity shows such as 'Pop Idols' are indicative of what
folk aspire to (neither is it insignificant that the term 'idol'
is used). But when such lives are looked at more closely,
a darker, sadder side is often revealed linked to a loss of
purpose and direction. One may think of the international
comic actor Peter Sellers, star of the lucrative and side-
splitting *Pink Panther* movies. He lived a glamorous and yet
tormented and selfish life. His friend and fellow 'Goon', Spike
Milligan, said of him, 'To try to know him was like going to
a desert island. He's that lonely. He's desperate to be happy,
successful, wanted, happily married. He's desperate not to
destroy his past. It's all desperation. He *is* desperation.'[7]

In a 'universe without windows', to use a phrase of Peter
Berger, one which is to be conceived in purely materialistic
terms, morality all but disappears. Dr Michael Ruse in his
book, *Taking Darwin Seriously* writes: 'The point about
morality is that it is an adaptation to get us to go beyond
regular wishes, desires and fears, and to interact socially with
people ... In a sense, therefore, morality is a collective illusion
foisted upon us by our genes. Note, however, that the illusion
lies not in the morality itself but in its objectivity.'[8] Ruse
is saying that morality always carries a feeling of 'ought'—
that is where its persuasive power comes from. There is,
however, no objective grounding for this 'ought' for there
is no God or transcendent source of value in which it may

7. Quoted by Roger Lewis in, *The Life and Death of Peter Sellers* (Arrow, 1995).
8. M. Ruse, *Taking Darwin Seriously*, (Oxford: Blackwell, 1986) p 253.

be rooted. Within a purely Darwinian paradigm our genes simply play a trick on us so as to ensure the survival of the species through what Ruse calls 'reciprocal altruism' whereby the reproductive success of an individual is increased by helping others. For instance, if I see someone drowning, I may feel compelled to dive in to help them. The underlying and unconscious gene-driven reason being that one day someone might do the same for me. It is not that there is an objective imperative which compels me to act in this way. Or it works by what Ruse calls 'kin selection'. Here the point being that we feel a stronger sense of moral obligation to those of the same blood because this will ensure the passing on of our family genes. The upshot of this approach is that morality which has always been considered to be objectively grounded in transcendent values (guaranteed by God) effectively vanishes into thin air.

Such a reductionist neo-Darwinian view of reality which evicts God from his universe has consequences for the value of human life too. Peter Singer in his book *Practical Ethics*,[9] takes as his starting point what he calls 'the principle of equal consideration of interests'. This is the position that the interests of all human beings must be taken into account when assessing the consequences of an action. He argues that this principle extends to other sentient beings who can suffer and only such beings can be said to have 'interests'. He puts forward the idea that humans can be thought of in two ways: as belonging to the species *Homo sapiens*, or being a person. He defines a person as a 'self-conscious or rational being'

---

9. Peter Singer, *Practical Ethics* (Cambridge: CUP, 1993), pp. 88, 169, 171–72.

who can therefore act as an agent in making decisions. Singer wants to maintain that some primates are also self-conscious to some extent and so could be described as persons. Being a member, therefore, of the *species* Homo sapiens is not a sufficient or necessary reason for being considered a person. This has very far-reaching implications. It means that adult primates are persons but a newborn human infant is not. It is therefore not intrinsically wrong to kill a newborn baby who is not self-conscious whereas it *would* be wrong to kill an animal who is supposedly self-conscious. Singer doesn't suggest that newborn children *should* be killed if they are healthy and wanted, but that they *could* be if they weren't. He argues that strict conditions should be placed on permissible infanticide, but that 'these restrictions might owe more to the effects of infanticide on others than to the intrinsic wrongness of killing an infant'. Singer admits that, 'If these conclusions seem too shocking to take seriously, it may be worth remembering that our present absolute protection of the lives of infants is a distinctively Christian attitude rather than a universal ethical value.'[10]

Losing God therefore entails a lot more than a loss in church attendance!

What, then, does our world begin to look like when God becomes 'weightless'—replaced by idols?

This is how Professor David Wells describes it,

---

10. Ibid. p. 172.

It is one of the defining marks of our time that God is now weightless. I do not mean by this that he is ethereal but rather that he has become unimportant. He rests upon the world so inconsequentially as not to be noticeable ... Those who assure the pollsters of their belief in God's existence may nonetheless consider him less interesting than television, his commands less authoritative than their appetites for affluence and influence, his judgement no more awe inspiring than the evening news, his truth less compelling than the advertisers' sweet fog of flattery and lies. That is weightlessness.[11]

This claim does not conflict with the findings of opinion polls carried out on both sides of 'the pond' which seem to reveal a good deal of interest in what is referred to as 'spirituality' or what Grace Davies refers to as 'believing without belonging'[12] as Wells goes on to argue, 'My comments on the weightlessness

---

11. David F. Wells, *God in the Wasteland*, p. 88.

12. 'What is clear is that most surveys of religious belief in northern Europe demonstrate continuing high levels of belief in God and some of the more general tenets of the Christian faith but rather low levels of church attendance' cited in Rodney Stark and Roger Finke, *Acts of Faith: Explaining the Human Side of Religion*, (Berkeley: University of California Press, 2000), p. 72. Wells draws attention to the downside of this for the church, 'In a study that was done in Britain in 2000 ... it was discovered that during approximately the final decade of the twentieth century, regular attendance at church dropped from being a practice of 28% of the population down to 8%. During this time, however, those who described themselves as spiritual, or who had spiritual experiences, rose from 48% to 76% ... It is not clear from this study itself whether the sharp rise in spiritual experience reflects the fact that people are being more spiritual or that they have become more willing to talk about it, but either way there is a belief that there needs to be a spiritual component to life, and one that the Church is not the place to find it.' David F Wells, *No Place for Truth or Whatever Happened to Evangelical Theology* (Grand Rapids: Eerdmans, 1993), p. 114.

of God ... focus on his *objective* significance—a matter of truth rather than psychology. I am talking about our relationship with God as the unchanging norm of what is true and right in all places, times, and cultures, a God whose reality is unaltered by the ebb and flow, the relativity of life, unaffected by private perceptions or internal psychology. In the crude language of our commercial culture, if God is objectively true, then he has the same cash value for all people, in all times, in all cultures.'[13]

What Wells depicts here might be an accurate description of the way God rests on your life if the truth be known. Or perhaps it describes the direction you find yourself drifting towards even as a Christian believer. If so, this is where Isaiah 44 comes to our aid as a necessary corrective.

The futility of idolatry

The prophet is not coy in pointing out the wastefulness of idolatry, v9, 'All who make idols are nothing and the things they treasure are worthless [profitless]. Those who would speak up for them are blind; they are ignorant to their own shame.'

When it is claimed that those who make idols are 'nothing' it is another way of saying that they haven't a clue about the purpose of life and are therefore clueless of how to go about finding it.[14] The things they treasure, or as one translation

---

13. David F. Wells, *God in the Wasteland* p. 91.

14. 'The meaning here is that to fashion an idol proves that the maker has no sense of meaning and purpose in the world nor any chance of achieving it' Alec Motyer, *The Prophecy of Isaiah* (Leicester: Inter Varsity Press, 1993), p. 346.

puts it, 'their darlings'[15] is proof of that. What they invest their time and energy into making for themselves in order to give them some sort of meaning are 'worthless'—'empty'—that is, they simply don't provide what people are hoping for. What is more, those who are promoting these things should have known better, but in fact they are just showing up their own ignorance by their idol making activity.[16]

What are the kinds of 'darlings' that people today have bought into in the hope that they will fill the God-shaped vacuum in their souls? The list is endless.

We live in what is, in effect, a polytheistic society (that is a society with many gods) in that we give ourselves, with varying degrees of what can only be called idolatry, to the service of money making, career making, power grabbing, food, drink, fashion, entertainment, cars, gambling, sex and so on. This assertion does not imply that no man can give attention to these things without guilt. There is a due degree of attention that such things merit. But in fact they are getting *excessive* attention. As objects of concern they are attracting the kind and degree of human response more proper to the religious sphere. They have become objects of devotion.[17]

At the centre of them all is 'self', the self which wants to be

---

15. C. R. North, *Second Isaiah* (Oxford: OUP, 1964), p. 40.

16. 'The irony is that those who worship idols become as dead as the idols they worship, and those who inflame themselves in worship of them are consumed by the fires of judgement.' Wells, *God in the Wasteland*, p. 53.

17. Blamires, op. cit. p. 122.

satisfied and the self which thinks it has the power to do it all by it*self*.

It is the assertion of self over and against God which defines sin as lawlessness (1 John 3:4) which in turn fuels the drive towards idolatry.

Why do people choose the substitute over God himself? Probably the most important reason is that it obviates accountability to God. We can meet idols on our own terms because they are our own creations. They are safe, predictable, and controllable; they are, in Jeremiah's colourful language, the 'scarecrows in a cucumber field' (10:5). They are portable and completely under the user's control. They offer nothing like the threat of a God who thunders from Sinai and whose providence of this world so often appears to us to be incomprehensible and dangerous.[18]

Little wonder that Isaiah in particular engages in a systematic attack on idolatry as deluded and deluding.

The foolishness of idolatry

Neither is Isaiah reticent about spelling out the utter folly of idolatrous living, verses 10–19.

Who shapes a god and casts an idol,
        which can profit nothing?
People who do that will be put to shame;
        such craftsmen are only human beings.

---

18. Wells, *God in the Wasteland*, p. 53.

Let them all come together and take their stand;
> they will be brought down to terror and shame.

The blacksmith takes a tool
> and works with it in the coals;

he shapes an idol with hammers,
> he forges it with the might of his arm.

He gets hungry and loses his strength;
> he drinks no water and grows faint.

The carpenter measures with a line
> and makes an outline with a marker;

he roughs it out with chisels
> and marks it with compasses.

He shapes it in human form,
> human form in all its glory,
> that it may dwell in a shrine.

He cut down cedars,
> or perhaps took a cypress or oak.

He let it grow among the trees of the forest,
> or planted a pine, and the rain made it grow.

It is used as fuel for burning;
> some of it he takes and warms himself,
> he kindles a fire and bakes bread.

But he also fashions a god and worships it;
> he makes an idol and bows down to it.

Half of the wood he burns in the fire;
> over it he prepares his meal,
> he roasts his meat and eats his fill.

He also warms himself and says,
> 'Ah! I am warm; I see the fire.'

From the rest he makes a god, his idol;

he bows down to it and worships.
He prays to it and says,
    'Save me! You are my god!'
They know nothing, they understand nothing;
    their eyes are plastered over so they cannot see,
    and their minds closed so they cannot understand.
No one stops to think,
    no one has the knowledge or understanding to say,
'Half of it I used for fuel;
    I even baked bread over its coals,
    I roasted meat and I ate.
Shall I make a detestable thing from what is left?
    Shall I bow down to a block of wood?'

What is striking about this description of idol making is the centrality of human *effort*; v. 12 'The *Blacksmith* takes a tool and works it with coals'; v. 13, 'The *carpenter* measures with a line and makes an outline with a marker'; v. 14, '*He* cuts down cedars or perhaps took a cypress or oak' to make the idol. Man by his own ingenuity and skill is able to produce (so he thinks) something which is going to give him value and worth and, indeed, according to verse 17, 'salvation.'

What can people look to which they feel they can manufacture which will, in some way, 'save' them?

In *Culture and the Death of God*, literary critic Terry Eagleton lists several idols of the modern age. He points out that Enlightenment rationalists made a god out of reason; Romantics deified the imagination; nationalists exalted the nation; and Marxists offered an economic analysis of sin and salvation. 'Not believing in God is a far more arduous affair than is generally imagined' is the conclusion Eagleton comes to, 'When God is rejected something else must be concocted to replace him'.[19]

To what kind of 'God-substitutes' do people turn?[20]

Some look to philosophy, man's unaided reason to make sense of life without God. One person who tried this was Bertrand Russell. In 1910 he wrote a book which, as an atheist, he called 'his gospel'. The title of the book was, 'A Free Man's Worship' which was to become the manifesto of humanism in the 20th century. Having argued that we are nothing but 'the outcome of an accidental collocations of atoms', he came to this bleak conclusion, that 'all the labours of the ages, all the devotion, all the inspiration, all the noonday brightness of human genius are destined to extinction in the vast death of the solar system, and that the whole temple of Man's achievement must inevitably be buried beneath the debris of a universe in ruins.' *Everything*, all our achievements and families are going to disappear into the black hole of nothingness one day. That's it!

---

19. Terry Eagleton, *Culture and the Death of God* (New Haven, CT: Yale University Press, 2014) p. 119.

20. The term God-substitutes is one used to great effect by Tim Keller who writes, 'Every human personality, community, thought-form, and culture will be based on some ultimate concern or some ultimate allegiance—either to God or to some God substitute … The best way to analyse cultures is by identifying their corporate idols.' 'Talking about Idolatry in a Postmodern Age,' Gospel Coalition, April 2007, http://christianlibrary.org.au/index.php?option=com_content&view=article&id=131:talking-about-idolatry-in-a-postmodern-age&catid=41:school-of-preaching&Itemid=73.

Given what happened four years later with the Armageddon called 'The Great War' one could be justified in thinking Russell had a point. But of course World War 1 and World War 2 might be given a different interpretation, namely, that that is precisely where you end up when human beings reject God and run after idolatries—a 'feeding on ashes', v20.

While some serve philosophies to find purpose, others serve possessions. Churches may be empty but the DIY stores are full. Cathedrals may be falling down but shopping malls are going up. Chapels may be shrinking but sports stadiums are expanding. Don't get me wrong, home improvement, entertainment and physical fitness are fine in themselves but become twisted when they receive the devotion rightly reserved for God in consuming our time and money, until the consumer himself becomes consumed.

The folly is in thinking that it is possible to make from things which are *less* than human something which is *more* than human in order to give humans the power they need to make it through life without God—v. 13, 'The carpenter measures with a line and makes an outline with a marker; he roughs it out with chisels and marks it with a compass. He shapes it into the form of a man, a man in all his glory.' When God has been shunted into the sidelines of our thoughts and so becoming 'weightless', then the highest thing man can think of is himself for what else is there? But then what he attempts to make as an object of worship is in the end *less* than himself with the consequence that in giving himself over to it he *debases* himself as Isaiah highlights in v. 15b 'he makes an idol and bows down to it.'

It simply doesn't make sense to think that it is possible to make from mere 'stuff', something which is going to provide supernatural power, v. 19, 'No one stops to think, no one has the knowledge or understanding to say, "half of it I used for fuel; I even baked bread over its coals, I roasted meat and ate. Shall I make a detestable thing from what is left? Shall I bow down to a block of wood?"' 'Look' the prophet is in effect saying, 'God has given us lots of good things in life to enable us to live, things like wood from which you can make a fire to warm yourself and cook your food. But it is sheer stupidity in the extreme to then try and make from the leftovers, something which only *God* can give you—value and worth.'

In the 21st century West we may not be busy carving out statues to worship from pieces of wood, but we do the same thing in other ways. For example, God has given us families in which we are meant to learn how to relate to each other as human beings and so flourish. But when those children or grandchildren or even parents, become the things which we live *for* and *from* which we feel we gain our significance— our reason for existing—then we have made them into idols just as surely as a pagan in Babylon made a god out of lump of wood. That which is good then becomes corrupt and corrupting. Here we have the manipulative mother who will not let her children grow up or leave the nest, but will always be 'feeling ill' so that the children will be forever tied to her apron strings and be perpetual spinsters or bachelors. A good thing—family—which God has given becomes a bad thing when we abuse it because the self wants to be in control rather than God.[21]

The same can happen within churches. This occurs when an appeal is made to self and felt needs being King rather than God and his truth. It is quite possible, for example, to have church growth which is not Gospel growth. It is straightforward and simple really, all you have to do is to take that which is good in its own sphere, like marketing strategy in business, and apply it to where it shouldn't be applied, namely the church, and you will get growth. The maxim is, 'give the punters what they want'.

Here is an example of such an approach taken from a book on church growth:

> The church is a business. Marketing is essential for a business to operate successfully. The Bible is one of the world's great marketing texts. However, the point is indisputable: the Bible does not warn against the evils of marketing. So it behoves us not to spend time bickering about techniques and processes. Think of your church not as a religious meeting place, but as a service agency—an entity that exists to satisfy people's needs. The marketing plan is the Bible of the marketing game; everything that happens in the life of the product occurs because the plan wills it. It is critical that we keep in mind

---

21. The hellish effects of this kind of behaviour has been skilfully portrayed by C. S. Lewis in his *The Great Divorce* (Zondervan, 2000) pp. 97–115.

the fundamental principle of Christian communication: the audience, not the message, is sovereign.[22]

This means that if people don't like talk of 'sin', then such talk must be cut out. If people want to be told that God is always for them and makes no demands upon them, then all challenge will be removed from the sermon (if there is a sermon at all).

Some churches have decided to go down this route, replacing exposition with entertainment. The largest church in the USA is in Houston, Texas, with a membership of forty thousand. The Pastor, Joel Osteen, regularly teaches what he has written in his best selling book, *Your Best Life Now* (even the title gives the game away) There are seven steps, he says, to 'living at your full potential': 1. enlarge your vision; 2. develop a healthy self-image; 3. discover the power of your thoughts and words; 4. let go of the past; 5. find strength through adversity; 6. live to give; 7. choose to be happy. This amounts to little more than wrapping up the American dream in Christian dress and selling it as the real deal. Of course thousands are going to go and hear such teaching for that is what they *want* to hear. Some churches in the UK do the same, maybe on a smaller scale, but it is the same error— placing man at the centre and pushing God to the margins so that he becomes weightless.[23]

---

22. George Barna, *Marketing the Church* (Navpress, 1988).

23. 'The argument here is that in many respects ours is not a sceptical age so much as a superstitious age. This statement is based not only on the widespread growth of cults like those of the Moonies and the Scientologists, but on the switching of human veneration toward a thousand new idols. The cults

This tendency to replace God, and so lose him, in the church in response to the market, is summarised by Wells,

> God is much friendlier, too. Gone are the notes of judgement, though these are more displaced than denied, and they are replaced by those of love and acceptance ... Sin is preached but is presented more in terms of how it 'harms the individual, rather than how it offends a holy God. Sin, in short, prevents us from realizing our full potential.' Conversion is insisted upon but then, paradoxically, it is the this-worldly benefits that are accentuated, the practical benefit of knowing Christ receiving all the attention with scarcely a look at what happens if we turn away from him.[24]

The fatality of idolatry

There is a price to be paid for idolatry however, and it is fatal, v. 20, 'He feeds on ashes, a deluded heart misleads him; he cannot save himself or say, "Is not this thing in my hand a lie?"'

The Bible testifies and experience confirms that to put anyone or anything in the place of God results in disaster.

---

are superstitions consciously chosen—even if their choice is irrational and made under mental duress. The idolatries are superstitions slid in by accident—the accident of making some human or material agency the pole star of mental orientation, of guiding purpose and incessant concern. This is called an "accident" in that the human or material agency is genuinely deserving of human attention and respect (as the cults are not), and the slide into that excess which involves servitude is not humanly foreseen.' Blamires, *Where do we stand?* p. 122.

24. David F. Wells, *Above all earthly pow'rs* (Grand Rapids, MI: Eerdmans, 2006), p. 306.

Our hearts are so misguided that we genuinely think that we can find satisfaction, morality and purpose without God, but at the end of the day all we are left with is the nasty taste of ashes in our mouths. For decades now our young people have been bombarded with so many different idols whereby it is claimed they can 'achieve their potential'—through fashion, career, fame, and sex, but the social experiment has been seen to have failed except by the most dewy-eyed liberals. The gods we have been so busily pursuing and offering to our children have failed us (and more tragically—them). The sense of well-being promised is not lasting and the idols are exacting their price with a vengeance.

Let us take one example: psychosocial disorders amongst young people.

Twenty years ago Sir Michael Rutter, Professor of Child and Adolescent Psychiatry in London and David Smith, Professor of Criminology in Edinburgh, published a massive study[25] which focused on disorders that are increasing in teenage years—crime, suicide, depression, anorexia, bulimia, alcohol and drug abuse. What was striking was that a major increase in these problems occurred in the golden era of low unemployment and rising living standards between 1950 and 1973. In Britain recorded crime amongst the young had increased tenfold from 1950–1993. So had alcohol consumption and alcohol-related behaviour problems, as well as depressive disorders.

---

25. Sir Michael Rutter (Editor), David J. Smith (Editor) *Psychosocial Disorders in Young People: Time Trends and Their Causes* (Wiley, 1995).

What are the causes?

The authors agreed that those amongst the poor and those living on the 'sink estates' are more *likely* to be criminal, depressed etc., than those in more comfortable surroundings and yet it can't account for the rise in these problems amongst young people in general, because the rise was the most marked during the period of *prosperity*. The West has been fed the lie that material well-being equals spiritual/ social well-being—it does not. We are made for something more, indeed, made for *someone* more and that someone is God. Not the god of our imagination but the God of glory, so powerful and so personal he is able to save us and put us back on track towards him.

That is the conclusion in v. 21ff as God makes a heart-rending appeal to his people through his prophet, 'O Israel I will not forget you. I have swept away your offenses like a cloud, your sins like the mist of the morning. Return to me for I have redeemed you.' Isn't that wonderfully reassuring? *We* may forget God, but *he* will not forget us. When God occupies his rightful place, as we realise he has dealt with our sins by removing them from his presence through his Son's death on the cross (Isaiah 53), and we return to him so that he becomes the centre of our thoughts and his goals become our goals in life, then everything else begins to fall into its rightful place. The things he has made, the stars in the heavens, or the trees in the forest which were never meant to be worshipped, suddenly testify to the one who is *to be* worshipped, v. 23, 'Sing for joy, O heavens for the Lord has done this; shout aloud, O earth beneath. Burst into song, you mountains, you forests and all your trees for the Lord has redeemed Jacob, he displays his glory (weight) in Israel (church).'

Here we see the freedom which the true God offers in contrast to the slavery of idolatry. The Christian can celebrate the joy of sex, not as an end in itself but as a God-given gift for the mutual enrichment of husband and wife within marriage. Music can be enjoyed not as a mindless master but as a wonderful gift of the Creator who causes the very heavens to sing. Food is not to be greedily consumed but received with thanksgiving. These are truths the redeemed know and are to proclaim, and as they do, with Jesus Christ being the centre of their lives, the weight of the Lord is then displayed amongst his people.[26]

---

26. 'In one sense idolatry is the diagnosis of the human condition to which the gospel is the cure. At root, the problem with humans is not horizontal 'social' problems (like sexual immorality and greed), but rebellion against and replacement of the true and living God with gods that fail (which leads to these destructive sins). If the story of the human race is a sorry tale of different forms of idolatry, the height of human folly, the good news is that God reconciles his image-bearers back to himself in Christ. It is no accident that the prophets envisage a time when idols will ultimately be eradicated and replaced by true worship.' Rosner, op. cit., p. 29.

2

When God is Replaced

The Problem of Pride, Ezekiel 28

Why is the world in a mess? That was a question which produced a considerable amount of correspondence in the London Times newspaper many years ago. The most penetrating and succinct answer was given by the Christian writer, G. K. Chesterton: 'What's wrong with the world?' the editor asked. The reply came, 'Dear Sir, I am. Yours sincerely, G. K. Chesterton'. What is the heart of the problem of evil which stalks our world with its suicide bombings, muggings, sexual abuse and anti-social behaviour? The Bible's answer is that it is the human heart.

Perhaps nowhere is this better illustrated than Ezekiel Chapter 28 and the tragedy of the King of Tyre, which, as we shall see, is also your tragedy and mine.

Man's Folly

At the very beginning of the prophetic oracle, Ezekiel pinpoints the locus of the problem: vv. 1–5,

> The word of the LORD came to me: 'Son of man, say to the ruler of Tyre, "This is what the Sovereign LORD says: 'In the pride of your heart you say, "I am a god; I sit on the throne of a god in the heart of the seas." But you are a man and not a god, though you think you are as wise as a god. Are you wiser than Daniel? Is no secret hidden from you? By your wisdom and understanding you have gained wealth for yourself and amassed gold and silver in your treasuries. By your great skill in trading you have increased your wealth, and because of your wealth your heart has grown proud.'"'

In the figure of the King of Tyre we have the epitome of pagan man. It soon becomes apparent that this paradigm pagan man has an enormous self-esteem problem, namely, the problem of an enormous self-esteem! God says, 'Your heart has grown *proud.*' The fact is that the Bible sees the problem of high self esteem to be much more serious and far more dangerous than the problem of low self-esteem. The question which immediately comes to mind is: Where did the King of Tyre get his high self-esteem from? According to verses 4–5 it flowed from his great achievements. By *his* wisdom and understanding (so he thinks) he has amassed 'great wealth' and because of his great wealth, we are told, his heart 'has grown *proud.*'

Here, then, is the self-made man *par excellence.* Rupert Murdoch has nothing on this fellow! We have to realise that

Tyre at this time was a very prosperous and highly influential city state. Therefore, when we hear the word 'Tyre', we are to think: 'Washington', 'Bonn', or 'London'. This means that this King was a major 'mover and shaker' on the political world-scene and what is more, he knew it. He was successful and secure; prosperous and proud. And, as far as he was concerned, he had every reason to be.

This was the outlook which dominated most of the 20th century and is still very much with us in the 21st century. It is the maxim of the 5th century BC Greek philosopher, Protagoras, that 'Man is the measure of all things.' It is the promethean arrogance of Leon Battista Alberti during the Renaissance who declared 'A man can do all things if he will.' It is the optimistic humanism of President Kennedy's inaugural address: 'since most of the world's troubles have been caused by man most of the problems can be solved by man.'

Not that much has changed.

The predominant view abroad is that with the right knowledge, the right resources, and the right will, crime on our streets will be reduced, terrorists will be hunted down and brought to account, poverty will be abolished and our environment made safe.

Undoubtedly as human beings we have achieved so much. But herein lies the danger, namely, that of being seduced into thinking that it is by our achievements that we measure our self-worth and thus bolster our self-confidence.

You may say, 'What's wrong with that? We all want to achieve something—good exam results, a happy marriage, a peaceful society, even a successful church.' Of course in and of itself there is nothing wrong with achievement as such. It is better to achieve rather than fail to be sure. But this drive for achievement rarely exists 'in and of itself' because such aspirations are often poisoned by pride. This is the real problem and besetting sin of the human race as exemplified by the King of Tyre. It is the myth of *self*-achievement, *self*-sufficiency, *and self*-aggrandisement. The trap is that such thinking invariably excludes God because our focus is on self. As a result we begin to home in too much on ourselves so that it is *our* wants, *our* plans, *our* feelings which begin to fill our horizon and God is squeezed to the periphery and so again becomes weightless. In short, we begin to see ourselves as gods—independent and autonomous with no one more ultimate than ourselves. When challenged about something we have decided to do, against the advice of others, don't we defensively respond with: 'Well, it's *my* life; *I* will do with it what *I* want.'? In some cases this is even encouraged, 'Believe in yourself; you can do whatever you want to do, be whatever you want to be', we are told. Not so much the power of positive thinking but the folly of wishful *un*thinking. It is when we have achieved much, especially by amassing wealth and all the power and prestige which accompanies it, that the delusion is fed that *we* are in control, as we think, 'If I have done *this*, then what is to stop me achieving more in the future? *I* am the master of my fate, the captain of my soul.'

However, the real trouble comes when we move from thinking that we are gods, with a small 'g'—v. 2, to *acting* as if we were 'gods' This doesn't mean that we go around shouting, 'I am god, I am god!' like children in the school playground running around saying, 'I am Spiderman'! But the behaviour we often display reveals that deep seated inclination, the view that *we* occupy the centre of our horizons even in the small things of life. To take a trivial example: suppose someone were to produce an old group photograph of your Primary school class. Who does your eye immediately start searching for? Is it not yourself? We immediately ask, 'Where am *I* in this picture?' That may be a fairly innocuous and mild expression of how egotistical most of us are, but with some people it goes even further and with catastrophic results.

Take the case of the artist Pablo Picasso.

In her book, *'Life with Picasso'*, Françoise Gilot, who was forty years younger than Picasso, tells the story of her ten years as his third mistress. She said that for him there were only two kinds of women—goddesses and doormats—and sooner or later everyone went from the first category to the second. Gilot once told him he was 'the devil'—whereupon Picasso branded her with a cigarette held to her cheek, only stopping because, as he put it, 'I may still want to look at you.' Picasso once said that, 'When I die, it will be a shipwreck, and as when a huge ship sinks, many people all around will be sucked down with it.' After he died in 1973 (aged 91), his second wife Jacqueline, an early mistress Marie-Thérèse, and grandson Pablito committed suicide. Several others had mental breakdowns including his first wife, Olga, and his most famous mistress Dora Maar. His mother warned his first wife, 'I don't believe any woman could be happy with my son. He's available only to himself.'

What has any of this to do with the claim that we act as if we were god? In this way: Picasso believed he had the right to do whatever he wanted with whomever he wanted if he was powerful enough. He was powerful and so he did what he wanted. That is, his behaviour was linked to his beliefs which were atheistic. Picasso was an avowed follower of Nietzsche who claimed that 'God was dead' leaving only the 'will to power'. But if God is dead who is going to replace him? Picasso had the answer—himself. Who else was there? Indeed, one day, Gilot records that Picasso was heard muttering to himself, 'I am God, I am God'. That is the mindset of the King of Tyre and sadly, the natural mindset of all of us if only we had the audacity to voice it.

Of course modern man has now given way to postmodern man who, as a matter of principle, takes this a stage further. What that looks like is captured by this description given by Jeremy Rifkin,

> We no longer feel ourselves to be guests in someone else's home and therefore obliged to make our behaviour conform with a set of pre-existing cosmic rules. It is our creation now. We make the rules. We establish the parameters of reality. We create the world, and because we do, we no longer feel beholden to outside forces. We no longer have to justify our behaviour, for we are now the architects of the universe. We

are responsible to nothing outside ourselves, for we are the
kingdom, the power, and the glory for ever and ever.[1]

This defiance of the real God who lovingly gives us every
breath we take whilst continuing to live in his world as if he
were an irrelevance, can be traced back to the root of all sin
which is pride. It is this word which forms the two bookends
(what is called an *inclusio*) of this section, so we read in vv. 2,
'In the *pride* of your heart' and then in v. 5 'your heart has
grown *proud*'. We may wonder: Why is pride considered
to be such a big deal with God? Why doesn't God round
on the King of Tyre for his greed and cruelty for instance
which were legendary? The answer is that it is pride which
gives rise to these other things and expresses most vividly
the anti-God state of our hearts. If you want to know how
proud you are then ask yourself this simple question: 'How
angry do I get if I am snubbed or ignored?' If the answer is,
'Quite a lot', then you have a serious issue with self-esteem.
The problem, as C. S. Lewis observed, is that each person's
pride is in competition with everyone else's pride. Pride by its
very nature is competitive. It must have someone else to look
down on in order to thrive. To see that this is so, you only
have to ask: Why is it that an incredibly rich person wants to
get even richer? After all you can only enjoy a certain number
of cars, dresses, homes and so on. It is because in order to feel
really good (by feeling powerful), you have to be richer than
someone else. And on and on it goes: I must beat that person
in the exam, this person at sport—not because it is the aim of
the game, but because it makes me feel better knowing that

---

1. Jeremy Rifkin, *Alguien: A New Word—A New World* (Viking, 1983), p. 244.

there is always someone down there I can measure myself
against and that way I can feel like a god.

C. S. Lewis in his own inimitable way puts the matter like
this:

> Pride has been the chief cause of misery in every nation and
> every family since the world began. Other vices may sometimes
> bring people together; you may find good fellowship and jokes
> and friendliness amongst drunken people or unchaste people.
> But Pride always means enmity—it is enmity. And not only
> enmity between man and man, but enmity to God ... In God
> you come up against something which in every respect is
> immeasurably superior to yourself. Unless you know God as
> that-—you do not know God at all. As long as you are proud
> you cannot know God. A proud man is always looking down
> on things and people: and, of course, as long as you are looking
> down, you cannot see something that is above you.[2]

A moment's honest self-reflection soon reveals that sadly
Lewis is quite correct. The desire to be autonomous coupled
to the belief that we have the power to do so, inevitably leads
to action in an attempt to be so. The King of Tyre is not just
an old phenomenon—he is a universal phenomenon for he is
'Everyperson'.

God's verdict

What is God's assessment of such attempts at flagrant self-

---

2. C. S. Lewis, *Mere Christianity* (Fount, 1978), pp. 108–109.

autonomy? It is that it is *he* and not the King of Tyre who is God and will be seen to be God: vv. 6–10.

> Therefore, this is what the Sovereign LORD says: 'Because you think you are wise, as wise as a god, I am going to bring foreigners against you, the most ruthless of nations; they will draw their swords against your beauty and wisdom and pierce your shining splendour. They will bring you down to the pit, and you will die a violent death in the heart of the seas. Will you then say, "I am a god," in the presence of those who kill you? You will be but a man, not a god, in the hands of those who slay you. You will die the death of the uncircumcised at the hands of foreigners. *I have spoken*, declares the Sovereign LORD.'

We so easily deceive ourselves.

At the turn of the 20th century people really did believe that with science and technology at their disposal they were going to bring about paradise on earth. Blake's dream of building Jerusalem on 'England's green and pleasant land' was sung with gusto and conviction in our public schools. The result was that many of those young men were left dead, dying or maimed on the killing fields of Passchendaele and the Somme. The science which was going to save mankind and usher in a new era of unprecedented prosperity, simply devised more efficient ways of destroying people. On the first day of the Battle of the Somme 20,000 British troops were killed and 40,000 were injured. The 1914–18 war was going to be the 'war to end all wars', but within a short space of 20 years the world saw an even bloodier war and even greater atrocities. This time science was used to bring about the 'final solution' in the gas chambers of Auschwitz and Belsen. This too was a time when God was pushed out of the picture and the conceit of man blossomed without restraint.

It was not simply Christians who foresaw that these things would happen. Nietzsche saw modern Europe descending into a dark abyss and in his *Ecce Homo* in the 1880s warned, 'There will be wars such as have never happened on earth.' Similarly after the First World War, Franz Kafka wrote, 'The buttresses of human existence are collapsing. Historical development is no longer determined by the individual but by the masses. We are shoved, rushed, swept away. We are the victims of history.'[3]

In all of this we must not think that God was inactive. God hadn't passively vacated his rightful position as ruler of his world. Rather he was allowing the overweening pride of man to follow its logical course—as he was doing here with the King of Tyre—as if to say, 'You think that you can manage the world better without me, you are so wise, so proud and powerful, then go ahead, meet others who are also wise, proud and powerful and they will beat you.' Hitler said 'He was a god'—although he didn't look too much like a god as his charred remains were dragged out of the Reichstag bunker in 1945—v. 9, 'Will you then say, "I am a god," in the presence of those who kill you? You will be but a mortal, not a god, in the hands of those who slay you?' The truth is that none of us look very much like gods when we shake our puny

---

3. Quoted in Michael Harrington, *The Accidental Century* (Penguin Books, 1967), p. 31.

fists in defiance against the one who made us and loves us, as we think we can outsmart him and do a better job of running the world than he can. It is the outlook of the madhouse. But each time we think such a thing, and do such a thing (which we do daily), that is when we are following in the footsteps of the King of Tyre.

Man's tragedy vv. 11–19

The prophet now changes his tune, quite literally as he sings a song of lament which contrasts what the King previously was with what he has now become. Here are verses 12–17 from the NRSV, which is a better translation than the NIV in helping us to grasp the full meaning and import of the passage:

> Son of man, take up a lament concerning the king of Tyre and say to him: 'This is what the Sovereign LORD says: "You were the model of perfection, full of wisdom and perfect in beauty. You were in Eden, the garden of God; every precious stone adorned you: ruby, topaz and emerald, chrysolite, onyx and jasper, sapphire, turquoise and beryl. Your settings and mountings were made of gold; on the day you were created they were prepared. With an anointed cherub as guardian I placed you. You were on the holy mount of God; you walked among the fiery stones. You were blameless in your ways from the day you were created till wickedness was found in you. Through your widespread trade you were filled with violence, and you sinned. So I drove you in disgrace from the mount of God, and the guardian cherub drove you out from among the fiery stones. Your heart became proud on account of your beauty, and you corrupted your wisdom because of your splendour. So I threw you to the earth; I made a spectacle of you before kings."'

Who is Ezekiel referring to? It is the King of Tyre, he has already said so in verse 12. Then what is all this talk about 'Eden', and of being a 'model of perfection', 'blameless in all his ways' while 'living on the mountain of God'? By using poetic language, the prophet is trying to get his readers to realise that they are never going to understand the tragedy of the King of Tyre or the tragedy of their own lives unless they realise what humankind was like when originally created by God.[4]

When you think about it, what the prophet has related about the King of Tyre is *also* a description of Adam, God's ruler, in the Garden of Eden (Genesis 2 and 3). The King of Tyre, and indeed all of us, are children of Adam. This was the time when a man was truly King, the pinnacle of God's creation, made by God to live consciously in his presence and reflecting his glory as image bearer. The overall picture given in Genesis 2 is that of Adam being a Priest-King. He is a King who is to rule his little domain. But he is also a priest in that his work in the divine sanctuary of the Garden of Eden (the mountain of God) is meant to be an act of worship[5]. The tragedy of Genesis 3 is recast in Ezekiel 28 in terms of the King of Tyre to show that these are the heights from which we all have fallen.

The Bible views humans as being 'a little lower than the angels' according to Psalm 8. Now we view ourselves as a little

---

4. Ezekiel 28 together with Isaiah 14 are often taken as 'proof texts' for the 'fall of Satan', but the passages are almost certainly not teaching this view, see J.H. Walton, 'Serpent', in Alexander and Baker, *Dictionary of the Old Testament Pentateuch* (Inter Varsity Press, 2003), p. 738.

5. See Melvin Tinker, *Reclaiming Genesis* (Monarch, 2010).

higher than the apes, and in some cases much lower than they, because as far as we know apes do not rape or torture or devise all sorts of evil in their hearts as we do—vv. 15 and 16: 'wickedness is found in us ... we are filled with violence and we have sinned.' To be sure, the prophet is using poetic language to depict the utter desperation of the King of Tyre by linking his situation to Adam, and so we get a moving back and forth between the two—'walking amongst the fiery stones' whilst through his 'widespread trade' he is filled with violence. The vital point is this: we cannot really understand why the world is in such a mess, together with the mess of our individual lives, unless we see it as part of the bigger and much more tragic picture of humankind's devastating fall away from its Maker.

The Bible treads the delicate path between exalting man into a 'god' on the one hand and debasing him into a 'nothing' on the other. This balance has been well put by Blaise Pascal,

> I blame equally those who make it their sole business to extol man, and those who take on them to blame him, and those also who attempt to amuse him. I can approve none but those who examine his nature with sorrow and compassion ... It is dangerous to show man in how many respects he resembles the lower animals, without pointing out his grandeur. It is also dangerous to direct his attention to his grandeur without keeping him aware of his degradation. It is still more dangerous to leave him ignorant of both; but to exhibit both to him will be most beneficial ... How strange that Christianity should enjoin man to acknowledge himself worthless or even abominable, and at the same time aim at resembling his Maker. Without

the counterpoise which each of these injunctions forms to the other, his elevation would render him superlatively proud, or his abasement would render him dreadfully abject ... No doctrine could be more suitable for man than that which informs him of this two-fold capability into which he is always in danger of falling, despair and pride.'[6]

The King of Tyre tragedy which is the human tragedy, is the greatest tragedy in the universe and heaven weeps for us.

God's remedy

If this was all that God had to say, the tragedy would be even greater for we would have no hope. But God does have something else to say, through his Son, the Lord Jesus Christ.

Jesus as the King of Kings, through the deep tragedy of the cross, came to reverse the tragedy of the King of Tyre by bearing our tragedy in our place. This is how the apostle Paul put it in Philippians 2 (which we shall be looking at in greater detail in a later chapter),

> He did not consider equality with God something to be grasped at, but made himself nothing, taking on the very nature of a servant, being made in human likeness. And being found in appearance as a man, he humbled himself and became obedient to death, even death on a cross. Therefore, God exalted him to the highest place.

---

6. Blaise Pascal. *Thoughts on Religion and Philosophy* (translated Isaac Taylor, Edinburgh, 1894), pp. 9–10.

God does the exalting, not us.

Someone who discovered this for himself is the noted academic, Professor J. Budziszewski. This is how he relates his 'King of Tyre experience' prior to becoming a Christian in his *Escape from Nihilism*:[7] 'The main reason I was a nihilist, the reason that tied all these other reasons together, was sheer, mulish pride. I didn't want God to be God; I wanted J. Budziszewski to be God.' He goes on,

I have already noted in passing that everything goes wrong without God. This is true even of the good things he has given us, such as our minds. One of the good things I've been given is a stronger than average mind. I don't make the observation to boast: human beings are given diverse gifts to serve them in diverse ways. The problem is that a strong mind that refuses the call to serve God has its own way of doing wrong. When some people flee from God they rob and kill, others do a lot of drugs and have a lot of sex. When I fled from God I didn't do any of those things, my way of fleeing from God was to get stupid. Though it always comes as a surprise to intellectuals, there are some forms of stupidity that one must be highly intelligent and educated to achieve. God keeps them in His arsenal to pull down mulish pride and I discovered them all. That is how I ended up doing a doctoral dissertation to prove that we make up the difference between good and evil and we aren't responsible for what we do. I remember now that I taught those things to students. Now that is sin. It was also agony. I believed things that filled me with dread. I thought I was smarter and

7. J Budziszewski, 'Escape from Nihilism', www.undergroundthomist.org.

braver than the people who didn't believe them; I thought I saw an emptiness at the heart of the universe that was hidden from their foolish eyes. But I was a fool.

He then describes how he became a Christian:

How then did God bring me back? I came, over time, to feel a greater and greater horror about myself. Not exactly a feeling of guilt, not exactly a feeling of shame, just horror: an overpowering sense that my condition was terribly wrong. Finally it occurred to me to wonder why, if there were no difference between the wonderful and the horrible, I should feel horror. In letting that thought through, my mental censors blundered. You see, in order to take the sense of horror seriously and by now I couldn't help doing so I had to admit that there was a difference between the wonderful and the horrible after all. For once my philosophical training did me some good, because I knew that if there existed a horrible, there had to exist a wonderful of which the horrible was the absence. So my walls of self-deception collapsed all at once. At this point I became aware again of the Saviour whom I had deserted in my twenties. Astonishingly, though I had abandoned Him, he had never abandoned me. I now believe He was just in time. There is a point of no return, and I was almost there. I said I had been pulling out one component after another, and I had nearly got to the motherboard.

Why is the world in a mess? Because of us. Why is there hope for the world? Because of Jesus.

3

When God is Revealed

The need for the grandeur of God, Isaiah 40:1–31

It has been said by someone that 'the proper study of mankind is man'. I will not oppose the idea, but I believe it is equally true that the proper study of God's elect is God; the proper study of a Christian is the Godhead. The highest science, the mightiest philosophy, which can ever engage the attention of a child of God, is the name, nature, the person, the work, the doings, and the existence of the great God whom he calls his Father.

There is something exceedingly *improving to the mind* in a contemplation of the Divinity. It is a subject so vast, that all our thoughts are lost in its immensity; so deep, that our pride is drowned in its infinity. Other subjects we can compass and grapple with; in them we feel a kind of self-content, and go our way with the thought, 'Behold I am wise'. But when we come to this master-science, finding that our plumb-line cannot sound its depth, and that our eagle eye cannot see its height, we turn away with the thought that vain man would be wise, but he is like a wild ass's colt; and with solemn exclamation, 'I am but of yesterday, and know nothing'. No subject of contemplation will tend more to humble the mind, than thoughts of God ...

But while the subject *humbles* the mind, it also *expands* it. He who often thinks of God, will have a larger mind than the man who simply plods this narrow globe ... The most excellent study for expanding the soul, is the science of Christ, and him crucified, and the knowledge of the Godhead in the glorious Trinity. Nothing will so enlarge the intellect, nothing so magnify the whole soul of man, as a devout, earnest, continued investigation of the great subject of the Deity.

And, whilst humbling and expanding, this subject is eminently *consolatory*. Oh, there is, in contemplating Christ, a balm for every wound; in musing on the Father, there is a quietus for every grief; and in the influence of the Holy Ghost, there is a balm for every sore. Would you lose your sorrow? Would you drown your cares? Then go, plunge yourself in the Godhead's deepest sea; be lost in his immensity; and you shall come forth as from a couch of rest, refreshed and invigorated. I know nothing which can so comfort the soul; so calm the swelling billows of sorrow and grief; so speak peace to the winds of trial, as a devout musing upon the subject of the Godhead.[1]

Those are words preached by the then 20-year-old 19th

---

1. Quoted by J. I. Packer, *Knowing God* (Hodder, 1993), pp. 15–16.

century Baptist minister, C. H. Spurgeon. So eloquently put, the truth of what he says is penetratingly accurate. The fact is that wafer thin thoughts of God result in wafer thin Christianity. How a person thinks about God, argue Paul Froese and Christopher Bader in their book *America's Four Gods*,[2] is shaped by the answer to two questions. First, does God ever intervene in life? Second, does God ever make moral judgements about what we do and say? If the answer is 'yes', then we will have a very different faith from those who would answer, 'no'. In the case of the second group, God will be insipid, distant and dull, the God of 'moralistic therapeutic deism'. But if we really do believe God is as Spurgeon describes him to be—Triune, vigorous and active, then our world undergoes a radical transformation and things will never appear the same again.

The calling of the preacher

Traditionally in the church the main purpose of the minister's task of preaching is that under God this transformation happens. Three hundred years ago, Cotton Mather, a Puritan pastor in New England, described this task, 'The great design and intention of the office of a Christian preacher is to restore the throne and dominion of God in the souls of men.' This is why Biblically faithful sermons challenge as well as comfort; search the soul as well as restore the soul. Then it will be God, and not self, who occupies the throne of the soul.

This was the calling of the prophet Isaiah (Isaiah 6). God's

---

2. Ibid. p. 19.

people back then entertained the same kind of doubts about God that many in the church entertain today. They too questioned whether God ever intervened in life or made moral judgements about the way we live. It is right there in Isaiah 40:27, 'Why do you say, O Jacob and complain, O Israel, "My way is hidden from the Lord; my cause is disregarded by my God."' Isaiah looks forward to a time when God's people would be at the end of their tether, as herded off into Exile, they hang up their harps, and sit weeping by the rivers of Babylon, with Jerusalem being reduced to a charred ruin, a haunt for rats and jackals (Psalm 137). That is when the doubts would come flooding in: 'Is God *able* to help us? Does God *want* to help us?' Perhaps he can't, or worse still, perhaps he won't. That is what lies behind the complaint of verse 27—God is not able and God is not willing. So how are such doubts to be dealt with? God's proffered antidote is to replace meagre thoughts of God with mighty thoughts about him, so that, in the words of Spurgeon, our minds will be both' humbled' and 'expanded', resulting in 'consolation'.

The difficulty facing many in the church (not least because of the influence of the surrounding culture), is that God has been internalised. His transcendence has almost been forgotten with devastating implications,

> The external God has disappeared and has been replaced by the internal God. Transcendence has been swallowed up by immanence. God is to be found only within the self. And once that has happened, the boundary between right and wrong—at least as we had thought about these things—went down like a

row of falling skittles. Evil and redemption can be seen as two sides of the same coin, not the two alternatives to life.[3]

It would not be going too far to suggest that in some cases the self *becomes* god. The search for happiness and the satisfaction of self pretty much amount to much the same thing for many living in the West. How seriously misplaced such thinking is and how it needs to be replaced by correct thinking about God is set out by John Piper,

> Our fatal error is believing that wanting to be happy means wanting to be made much of. It feels good to be affirmed. But the good feeling is finally rooted in the worth of self, not the worth of God. This path to happiness is an illusion. And there are clues. There are clues in every human heart even before conversion to Christ. One of those clues is that no one goes to the Grand Canyon or to the Alps to increase his self-esteem. That is not what happens in front of the massive deeps and majestic heights. But we do go there, and we go for joy. How can that be, if being made much of is the centre of our health and happiness? The answer is that it is not the centre. In wonderful moments of illumination there is a witness in our hearts: soul-health and great happiness come not from beholding a great self but great splendour.[4]

In Isaiah 40 the prophet invites his readers to experience

---

3. David F. Wells, *God in the Whirlwind: How the Holy-Love of God Reorients Our World* (Crossway, 2014) p. 31.

4. John Piper, *God is the Gospel* (Crossway, 2005), p. 13.

great happiness and great soul health by displaying *great splendour* as he bids us, 'Behold your God!'

The God of consolation

This great chapter opens with the transcendent God comforting his people in an act of divine condescension, v. 1, 'Console, console my people, says your God. Speak tenderly to Jerusalem, and proclaim to her that her hard service has been completed, that her sin has been paid for, that she has received from the LORD's hand double for all her sins.' The prophet doesn't attempt to minimize the suffering God's people have experienced; he looks reality squarely in the face. Like slaves oppressed by a cruel tyrant they have endured what he calls a 'hard service'. But nonetheless his message is: 'Don't despair, for those long years of duress are now coming to an end. God certainly will not ignore your sins, in fact he will pay for them himself in a most remarkable way by sending his Servant to suffer as an atoning sacrifice (Isaiah 52–53)—that's the extent of his covenant love for you.[5] God is not bellowing at you in his wrath, but, like some young Romeo, speaking 'tenderly' to you, which is what verse 2 means, 'wooing' you. The double repetition of 'comfort, comfort' only adds emotional intensity to the voice of God. 'Your God, then, is a God of comfort—strengthening and

---

5. 'The development of this section of Isaiah will reveal that the 'period of duress' can be identified with the Babylonian captivity (43; 14) and the satisfactory payment with the sacrifice of the Servant of the LORD (52:13ff.). The central reality of the sacrifices guaranteeing their efficacy, was that they were a divine provision, from the LORD's hand, not human expedient' (Leviticus 17:11; cf. 53.6). J. A. Motyer, *The Prophecy of Isaiah. An Introduction and Commentary* (Downers Grove, IL: Inter Varsity Press, 1993), p. 299.

restoring and you are about to experience it', declares the prophet.

God has already summoned angelic messengers to prepare for his coming as we see in v. 3—'A voice of one calling: "In the desert prepare the way for the LORD; make straight in the wilderness a highway for our God."' A royal highway is to be constructed to carry the divine royal chariot. Far from having abandoned the people, the Lord their King is coming to them in order to lead them out of captivity. The prophet might well admit, 'You find it difficult to believe such things'. 'Hallelujah' is a word which does not come easily to your lips as you have been crushed under the heel of the oppressor. Nonetheless, I *want* you to believe it, for while it is true that we human beings are such ephemeral creatures, here today, gone tomorrow, who when the wrath of God breathes on us we wither away like dried leaves (v. 7), 'The grass withers and the flowers fall, because the breath of the LORD blows on them.' Whilst people are like grass there is one thing which is immune from the ravages of time and the vagaries of history and that is God's word of promise—"The grass withers and the flowers fall, *but the word of our God stands forever.*" (v. 8) '*That* is what I am asking you to put your faith in', urges the prophet—'not your feelings, nor your circumstances, but in the unchanging, dependable voice of God—"for the *mouth* of the Lord *has* spoken."'(v. 5). Like a shepherd, v. 11, the LORD comes to lead his flock from the barren desert wastelands into pastures they could never have dreamt of; gathering the little lambs into his arms, holding them close to his heart—that's how much his people mean to him. 'This is *glad* tidings (gospel)—v. 9—which is to be proclaimed from the mountaintops, the good news of God setting up his messianic kingdom of righteousness'. 'And *you*' declares the prophet, are invited to share in it, would you believe?

But that is the question of course, *would* they believe it? How can the prophet persuade them (and perhaps some of us), that they *must* believe it? The answer is that the only way to combat these low thoughts about God is to replace them with lofty thoughts about him. That is exactly what the prophet goes on to do in verse 12ff.

Comfort is to be found not in denying God's power and looking to our own resources, but in a massive reassertion of his absolute sovereignty over every twist and turn of our lives. The prophet does not excuse God (as proponents of the 'Openness of God' attempt to do), rather he exalts him. It is only against this backdrop of an all-knowing, all-powerful Creator-Redeemer God who 'sees the end from the beginning' (46:10), and who is intimately and passionately involved in the lives of his people, that the kind of faith can be elicited which can lift us out from the depths of despair. Certainly it is the case that sometimes God's purposes appear *inscrutable*—so we ask 'Why Lord are you allowing this?', but that doesn't mean they are *irrational*—having no purpose at all. There is a purpose, even if it is only known to God.

The God of creation

In this prophetic oracle a rhetorical question appears twice, once in v. 18 and then again in v. 25, 'To whom will you compare me?' asks God. Let us follow the prophet and see the results of such attempted comparisons. Let's ask: 'Where can we go in order to get some kind of handle on what God is *really* like?'

What about the arena of science and technology? Perhaps here we can find some insight into the nature of God?

We are so proud (and in many ways rightly so), of our knowledge and ability to harness the forces of nature for our own ends. But without wishing to underplay some of the most amazing achievements made through modern science, they really do pale into insignificance compared to what God is able to do. For example, would anyone like to try their hand at relocating the Pacific Ocean? Or redistributing the sand of the Sahara desert? Maybe someone might want to attempt to level off the Himalayas? Of course for humans such things are impossible, but not for God—v. 12ff, 'Who has measured the waters in the hollow of his hand, or who with the breadth of his hand marked off the heavens? Who has held the dust of the earth in a basket or weighed the mountains on the scales and the hills in a balance?' The answer is obvious: Yahweh, the LORD,

Even now scientists are reaching out to belief in God in order to comprehend and explain the phenomena of the universe. Here is Professor John Polkinghorne,

> In the early expansion of the universe there has to be a close balance between expansive energy (driving things apart) and the force of gravity (pulling things together). If the expansion dominated then matter would fly apart too rapidly for condensation of galaxies and stars to take place. Nothing

interesting could happen in so thinly spread a world. On the other hand, if gravity dominated, the world would collapse in on itself again before there was time for the processes of life to get going. For us to be possible requires a balance between the effects of expansion and contraction which at a very early epoch in the universe's history (the Planck time) has to differ from equality by no more than 1 in 10^{60}. The numerate will marvel at such a degree of accuracy. For the non-numerate I will borrow an illustration from Paul Davies of what that accuracy means. He points out that it is the same as aiming at a target an inch wide on the other side of the observable universe, twenty thousand million light years away, and hitting the mark.[6]

According to the prophet God hit the mark spot on! Such probabilities are nothing to him. Verse 12 literally reads, 'He adjusted the heavens with the span of his fingers'. As a man might adjust a small picture hanging on the wall between his thumb and small finger (a 'span'), God does that with the whole universe![7]

---

6. John Polkinghorne, *One World* (SPCK, 1987), pp. 57–58.

7. In this sense the Christian world view has great explanatory power and provides the 'best fit' as has recently been argued with great skill by Professor Alister McGrath in his 2009 Gifford lectures. McGrath provides plenty of fascinating examples of "fine-tuning" in nature, instances of "surprising facts" (Charles Pierce) which require explanation, or potential "clues to the meaning of the universe" (C. S. Lewis). He concludes that, 'These are the pearls that need to be strung together in such a way that they make the most sense. A Christian vision of reality offers us a way of seeing things in which these observations are no longer surprising; if anything, they are to be expected.' Alister McGrath, 'Clues to the meaning of the Universe?'—The *2009 Gifford Lectures*, the University of Aberdeen.

Perhaps we should go to our universities to find some measure of God? Maybe the intelligentsia will be able to tell us what God is like? vv. 13–14, 'Who has understood the mind of the LORD, or instructed him as his counsellor? Whom did the LORD consult to enlighten him, and who taught him the right way? Who was it that taught him knowledge or showed him the path of understanding?' We might ask: 'Which firm of consultants at the University Science Park did God approach when he set about the ambitious project of creating a universe?' We have problems *understanding* the workings of the cosmos let alone designing it. But God has no such difficulties. From the smallest neutron to the largest nebula, from the flea to the elephant, God's creative genius envisaged them all in an *instant*. He didn't have to work things out like we do from premises to conclusions, 'If this, then that'. God just *knows*. He is omniscient. That is what the word means—'*all* knowing'. Even the great Albert Einstein once said, 'I feel like a man chained. If only I could be freed from my intellectual smallness.' There are no such conceptual limitations imposed upon God.

We might go on to ask: how does God size up in comparison to the climax of creation—humankind? The world population is now around 7 billion people. That amounts to considerable collective strength. Put all that wisdom, energy and power together and you would end up with something very impressive indeed. But how does it compare to God? We are told in verses 15–17. They are like 'dust' on a shelf which can be swept away with the brush of the forefinger. Or like a 'drop' of water falling from the lip of a bucket, so insignificant that it is hardly noticed. We are not meant to be intimidated by the nations. They are a negative quantity as far as God is concerned. They do not even begin to measure up to him.

But what of religion itself? Perhaps man-made gods might provide a bench mark by which to compare God? And so the prophet considers the religious imagination in order to see what happens when it is allowed to roam free to seek a God-comparison. This is the most ludicrous comparison of all according to verses 18–20, 'With whom, then, will you compare God? To what image will you liken him? As for an idol, a metalworker casts it, and a goldsmith overlays it with gold and fashions silver chains for it. A person too poor to present such an offering selects wood that will not rot; they look for a skilled worker to set up an idol that will not topple.'

People construct their *mental* images of God as well as their *metal* images. As we saw in chapter 1, the human heart is by nature an idol factory, and idolatry amounts to trusting in a God *substitute* which could be anyone or anything-money, power, prestige, relationships, the position of the stars and on and on and on it goes *ad infinitum*. It is not difficult to see why we would prefer an idol to the real God because then we think we don't have to give an account to it; we make idols with which we feel comfortable and safe, which firmly remain under *our* control. But they amount to nothing in the end and invariably fail us when the chips are down—especially towards the end of our lives when we begin to approach death. Think of the idolatry of work. No man is ever going to look back on his life and say, 'You know, I wish I had spent more time at the office.' They are idols which simply topple.

But maybe it is amongst the great and mighty we glimpse something god-like and say 'Yes, God is like that', after all, the Kings of Babylon were thought to be gods—v. 21–24: 'Do you not know? Have you not heard? Has it not been told you from the beginning? Have you not understood since the earth was founded? He sits enthroned above the circle of the earth, and its people are like grasshoppers. He stretches out the heavens like a canopy, and spreads them out like a tent to live in. He brings princes to naught and reduces the rulers of this world to nothing. No sooner are they planted, no sooner are they sown, no sooner do they take root in the ground, than he blows on them and they wither, and a whirlwind sweeps them away like chaff.' This is how these great men who seem to wield so much power over the nations, directing the course of human history—Hitler, Stalin, Putin, Obama—appear before God. He only has to blow on them as a man might blow on a candle and they are gone, leaving behind only a vague wisp of smoke as a reminder that they once existed.

It is not Prime Ministers and Presidents who are the real movers and shakers of history; it is Yahweh for he brings them to nothing. Israel desperately needed to hear and remember this because in the years following this prophecy they were going to be subject, politically speaking, to one nation after another—the Babylonians, the Persians, the Greeks and the Romans. And when you find yourself under the jackboot of an oppressive power again you are going to ask: 'Does God care?' (v. 27).

In all sorts of ways rulers try and trample down God's people, as for example in Myanmar (Burma) today. The

Karen people, a tribe which is 44% Christian, are dreadfully abused by the military regime there. Instead of using mine detectors, the military take Christian women and children from this tribe and force them to walk on ahead of the troops through suspected minefields so that they are the ones who are either killed or maimed first. That is what the rulers of this world do. And what does the Lord say? It is that they may have their day, their moment of power, but it will not last forever, whereas his people will. No regime can ever destroy you. They may take away your life but they cannot take away your soul.

The prophet leads us by the hand for one final attempt to get the measure of God by way of comparison and asks us to look up and gaze at the stars—v. 26, 'Lift your eyes and look to the heavens: Who created all these? He who brings out the starry host one by one, and calls them each by name. Because of his great power and mighty strength, not one of them is missing.'

There is nothing more humbling or more breathtaking than to stand looking up at the heavens beneath a star-studded sky. How vast it all is and how small we all feel! A number of years ago, the Christian astronomer, Professor David Block (who was inducted into the British Astronomical Society at the age of 19) gave a presentation at Witwatersrand University in South Africa explaining why he believed in a designed universe. He showed a slide of one hundred billion stars. He pointed out to his overawed audience that if they were to count one star per second they would be there for two and a half thousand years[8]. What does Isaiah say? God calls them out *each one* by name! 'That is your God, Israel' declares the prophet, 'the God *you* believe is powerless to help you!'

But there is another reason why the prophet refers to God's power over the stars, and that is because like some people today, the Babylonians believed that human destiny was determined by their position. The stars were seen as gods. Babylonian religion was an astral cult. But such an understanding is topsy-turvy; God is the one who rules the stars, not they that rule us. He is the one who moulds space and time itself as the arena for his artistry. Our life is not governed by blind fate, but by an all-knowing, personal, Creator-Redeemer God who has a loving purpose for each one of his people. The apostle Paul says something very similar in that magnificent passage at the end of Romans 8: 'In all these things we are more than conquerors through him who loved us. For I am convinced that neither death nor life, neither angels nor demons, neither the present nor the future, nor any powers, *neither height nor depth,* nor anything else in all creation, will be able to separate us from the love of God that is in Christ Jesus our Lord.' When he speaks of 'neither height nor depth'—he is referring to the position of the planets in the sky; in other words, he is subverting all astral religions Do we honestly think that walking under a ladder, breaking a mirror, even failing to 'say our prayers' is going to cut us off from God's covenant love? If so, then we do not know the God of the Bible.

---

8. Cited in Ravi Zacharias, *Can Man Live without God?* (Nashville: W Publishing, 1994) p. 85.

The challenge of Isaiah was re-presented by Blaise Pascal to the sceptics of his own day, as we might well re-present them to those in our own:

> Let man then contemplate the whole of nature in her full and lofty grandeur; let him turn his gaze away from the lowly objects that surround him; instead let him behold the dazzling light set like an eternal lamp to illumine the universe. Then let him see the earth as a mere point in comparison with the vast orbit described by the sun. Let him ponder the fact that this vast orbit is itself but a tiny speck compared with that described by the stars in their journey through the universe.

> If our vision was to stop there, however, let the imagination go beyond. It will become weary of conceiving things before nature is tired of producing them. For the whole visible world is an imperceptible atom in the ample bosom of nature. No idea can come close to realising it. It is no good trying to inflate our notions beyond unimaginable space, and yet be conceiving mere atoms in comparison with reality. For reality is an infinite sphere whose centre is everywhere and whose circumference is nowhere. In short, it is the greatest sensible indication of God's omnipotence that human imagination should lose itself in that very thought.

> Let man, returning to himself, consider what he is compared with the reality of these things. Let him regard himself as lost in this remote corner of the universe. And from the tiny cell where he lodges, within the universe, let him examine at their

true worth the earth, its kingdoms, human cities, and man himself. For what is man face-to-face with such infinitude?'[9]

This does not mean that man is reduced to nothing, for Pascal holds dearly to the Biblical view of man being made in God's image, 'Man is merely a reed, the weakest thing in nature but he is a thinking reed. There is no need for the whole universe to take up arms to crush him; a vapour, a drop of water, is enough to kill him. But, though the universe were to crush him, man would still be nobler than his destroyer, because he knows he is dying, knows the universe has advantage over him. But the universe knows nothing of this.'[10] And it is the smallness of man set against the grandeur of God which makes God's tender kindness towards us all the more remarkable and moving.

The God of restoration

We could spend the whole of our lives scanning the entire universe in vain to find one thing which even *begins* to approximate the God who has made himself known in Scripture. He is the *incomparable* one. 'But', says the prophet, 'your trouble O Israel, (and we might say, 'O Church') is that you have been so battered by circumstances and so seduced by the world's propaganda that you have forgotten that fact. You think that God is like *you*—fickle and feeble; no bigger than your highest thoughts about him (which, to be frank, are not all that great to begin with). It is because you have forgotten the overwhelming reality of God that you whine,

---

9. *A Mind on Fire* (ed. James Houston, Hodder and Stoughton, 1991), p. 138.
10. *A Mind on Fire* p. 144.

"My way is hidden from the LORD; my cause is disregarded by my God (v. 27). The reason why your problems seem so great is because your view of God is so small.' What is the remedy? vv. 28–31. 'Do you not know? Have you not heard? The LORD is the everlasting God, the Creator of the ends of the earth. He will not grow tired or weary, and his understanding no one can fathom. He gives strength to the weary and increases the power of the weak. Even youths grow tired and weary, and young men stumble and fall; but those who hope in the LORD will renew their strength. They will soar on wings like eagles; they will run and not grow weary, they will walk and not be faint.'

Young men will fall exhausted. Even the young Babylonian warriors that God's people in Isaiah's time were so afraid of would one day be rendered immobile by arthritis. By way of contrast the people of God have available to them a supernatural resource which keeps them going on to the end if only they would avail themselves of it. What is the means of access to that resource? Faith. So much of faith in this tragic, broken world of ours is made up of patience which the prophet teases out for us in these final verses. The immature think that the normal Christian life is soaring eagle-like, gliding on some super-spiritual thermal layer. Not so, contends the prophet. Faith is very much about patience. The climax of this prophecy is the ability to *walk* in the midst of the darkness of life and to trust in so great and glorious a God. This same God offers this same message to his people today—to trust him on the basis of his self-revelation and to discover that he is as good as his word.

4

When God is Crucified

The necessity of the Cross, Philippians 2:5–11

In 1993 an international conference was held in Minneapolis entitled, 'Re-imagine'. It called for women to dig deep into their own imaginations to create new images of God. Aruna Gnanadason of the World Council of Churches said that her God has nothing to do with the crucifixion. She claimed that the 'cruel and violent death of Christ on the cross sanctions violence against the powerless in society.' Delores Williams of Union Theological Seminary went even further, 'I don't think we need folks hanging on crosses and blood dripping and weird stuff ... we don't need atonement, we just need to listen to the god within.' The members of the conference went on to hold their own form of a communion service with milk and honey, chanting, 'Our mother, Sophia (female wisdom), we are women in your image. Sophia Creator God, let your milk and honey flow.'

Why do we think that not only can we imagine God as we want him or 'her' to be, but 'out-imagine' God? The liturgy used by these women expresses their beliefs quite well, but it is hardly earth shattering. It is precisely what you would expect such a group to come up with; it is so predictable and anodyne. Of course you get something similar when men use their imaginations in concocting a religion, but they tend to be of a more savage nature—like the myths of the Nordic gods for example. In contrast, when the 'imagination' of the real God goes to work, we end up with something which no human being would ever envisage in a thousand years. For God, as it were, imagines himself *into* the world he has made. That Word (*Logos*) became a reality some 2,000 years ago. And as is the case with all the greatest and most sublime religious truths, it is best captured, not in a statement, but in a song—the song of Philippians 2, which is the song of the Crucified God.[1]

---

1. 'Since Ernst Lohmeyer's study of Philippians 2:6–11 the scholarly consensus has been that this passage is a self-contained poetic unit. There is no evidence to suggest it was a later interpolation into the original letter, and most recent writers consider the hymn to have been composed independently of and prior to the writing of Philippians.' P. T. O' Brien, in P. T. O'Brien, *The New International Greek New Testament Commentary: The Epistle to the Philippians* (Eerdmans, 1991), p 198. Others, like Gordon Fee are not so sure that the designation of 'hymn' is correct, nonetheless he writes, 'Whether hymn or not, and I have considerable doubts here, one can scarcely miss the poetic and exalted nature of much of this. But neither, by calling it a hymn, should one miss the narrative character of the passage which begins with Christ's pre-existence, followed by his incarnation, including his death on the cross, and concludes with his (assumed) return to heaven as the exalted Lord of heaven and earth.' Gordon Fee in Gordon D. Fee, *The New International Commentary of the New Testament, Paul's Letter to the Philippians* W. B. Eerdmans, 1995), pp. 193–194. We take the view that this is a hymn or poem, but will emphasise the 'divine narrative' in three stages.

The divine descent

Speaking of the Lord Jesus Christ the hymn, begins in verse 5, 'Who, being in the form of God, did not consider equality with God something to be grasped, but emptied himself, taking the form of a slave, in the likeness of men, being found in the form of a man, he humbled himself becoming obedient to death.'

For millennia angels worshipped him. Cherubim in dazzling, white-hot brilliance attended him. New worlds and spiralling nebulae were created by him. The 'him' that is being referred to is God the Son.

His voice was the purest and most beautiful voice in heaven, the archangels would stop whatever they were doing and fall silent just to listen—he is the Word.

His love is the bottomless source of all love. It was the love which brought creatures into being with the self-same capacity to love as he loved. He named them 'man' and 'woman' for they were made in his image—the 'image of the invisible God' (Genesis 1:27; Colossians 1:15).

His status was nothing less than divine—'the form of God'.

To put it another way, he was equal in divinity with God the Father. All that belongs to the 'godness' of God, also belongs to this one called 'the Son'. Those big 'Omni' words—omniscience, omnipotence, omnipresence apply to him for he is the all-knowing, all-powerful, all-present deity.

The question all of this raises is: What was he going to do
with his privileged position? You may say, 'What else *can* he
do? He has it and so must use it. God is God, he can't *cease*
being God.' But this is where we are given a glimpse into an
aspect of God's character we would never have envisaged to
exist. For *this* God, the *true* God, chooses not to exploit his
divinity, but to display it differently. Whilst literally having
the divine right to remain in heaven, to cling onto his power
and prestige if you will, he exercises a different divine right—
the right to be humble, the right to change his form whilst not
ceasing to be God.

We are told in the song that he 'emptied' (*ekenōsen*)
himself. This does not mean that he emptied himself of
something; rather he emptied *himself* in the sense that he took
on something *to* himself—namely, human nature, the form
of a slave—the form of a man. His divine form was hidden
under the veil of his human form.[2] Occasionally that veil was

---

2. The verb '*ekenōsen*' might be better translated 'made himself of no
account'—see P. T. O' Brien, *The New International Greek New Testament
Commentary The Epistle to the Philippians* (Eerdmans, 1991), p. 217. B. B. Warfield
comments on the '*ekenōsen*' verb as follows: 'Paul, in a word, says here nothing
more than that our Lord, who did not look with greedy eyes upon His state of
equality with God, emptied himself, if the language may be pardoned, of Himself;
that is to say, in precise accordance with the exhortation for the enhancement of
which His example is adduced, that He did not look on His own things ... He took
the 'form of a servant,' and so was 'made in the likeness of men.' But His doing
this showed that he did not set overweening store by His state of equality with
God, and did not count Himself the sufficient object of all the efforts. He was not
self-regarding: he had regard for others. Thus he becomes our supreme example
of self-abnegating conduct.' B. B. Warfield, *The Person and Work of Christ*, ed.
Samuel G. Craig (Philadelphia: Presbyterian and Reformed, 1950), pp. 42–43. For
a helpful discussion on Warfield's insight into the Incarnation as expressed in

lifted, for example on the Mount of Transfiguration (Matthew 17:1-17). There for one brief moment the 'form of God', the visible splendour of the divine status of heaven,[3] shone with a blinding brilliance. But for the most part of his earthly life the veil remained firmly in place. In the words of the Danish philosopher, Søren Kierkegaard, Jesus was 'the divine *incognito*'. '*Veiled* in flesh the Godhead see, hail *incarnate* deity' wrote Charles Wesley and he got it absolutely right.

This is what is known as the 'incarnation', God becoming man.

How do you even begin to summarise the astonishing Christian claim that in Jesus of Nazareth God became a full, genuine human being? It is not all that easy, but C. S. Lewis once tried:

The Second Person in God, the Son, became human himself: was born into the world as an actual man—a real man of a particular height, with hair of a particular colour, speaking in

---

Philippians 2, see Carl R. Trueman, 'The Glory of Christ: B. B. Warfield on Jesus of Nazareth' in *The Wages of Spin* (Mentor, Christian Focus, 2004) pp. 103-128.

3. Richard Bauckham argues that this passage does not suggest any diminishing of Christ's divinity: '... the phrase *to einai isa theō* ('being equal with God', 'equality with God') ... there is no question here of either gaining or losing equality with God. The pre-existent Christ has equality with God; the issue is his attitude to it. He elects to express it, not by continuing to enjoy 'the form of God' (*morphē theou*), which is the visible splendour of the divine status of heaven, but by exchanging this glorious form for the humble status of the human form (*morphēn doulou*) on earth.' In Richard Bauckham, *Jesus and the God of Israel: God Crucified and Other Studies on the New Testament's Christology of Divine Identity* (Paternoster Press, 2008), pp. 206-207.

a particular language, weighing so many stone. The Eternal
Being, who knows everything and who created the whole
universe, became not only a man but before (that) a baby, and
before that a foetus inside a Woman's body. If you want to get
the hang of it, think how you would like to become a slug or a
crab.[4]

A Christian contemporary of Lewis at Oxford, and fellow
apologist for the Christian faith, Dorothy L. Sayers, was
equally forthright and literal in her understanding of the
incarnation of Christ:

The Christian faith is the most exciting drama that ever
staggered the imagination of man ... the plot pivots on a
single character, and the whole action is the answer to a single
central problem—What do you think of Christ? The Church's
answer is categorical and uncompromising, and it is this: That
Jesus Bar-Joseph, the carpenter of Nazareth, was in fact and in
truth ... the God by whom all things were made. His body and
brain were those of a common man; his personality was the
personality of God ... He was not a kind of demon pretending
to be human; he was in every respect a genuine living man. He
was not merely a man so good as to be 'like God'—he was God.
This is the dogma we find so dull—this is the terrifying drama
of which God is both victim and hero. If this is dull, then what
in Heaven's name is worthy to be called exciting? The people
who hanged Christ never accused him of being a bore—on the
contrary they thought him too dynamic to be safe. It has been
left to later generations to muffle up that shattering personality

4. C. S. Lewis, *Mere Christianity* (Fount, 1972), p. 152.

and surround him with an atmosphere of tedium. We have efficiently pared the claws of the Lion of Judah, certified him 'meek and mild', and recommended him as a fitting household pet for pale curates and pious old ladies. To those who knew him, however, he no way suggests a milk-and-water person; they objected to him as a dangerous firebrand ... He was emphatically not a dull man in his human lifetime, and if he was God, there can be nothing dull about God either.[5]

Had you seen Jesus in the street you would have passed him by as just another Jewish peasant with calloused hands, stained armpits and sore feet. Even when he spoke, his accent would have grated, having a distinct northern quality to it which was not all that refined or polished. For most of the earlier part of his adult life, he hung doors and carried wooden beams as a carpenter. Not exactly what we would have expected when divinity came to earth. And yet *at the same time*, unbeknown to any onlooker but known to his heavenly Father, he hung planets in their orbits and carried light beams across the galaxies.

Consider these words of the 4th century theologian, Athanasius, as he reflects upon this event, the 'Word becoming flesh': 'The Word was not hedged in by His body, nor did His presence in the body prevent His being present elsewhere as well ... At one and the same time—this is the wonder—as Man he was living a human life, and as Word he

5. Dorothy L Sayers, 'The Dogma is the Drama' in *Creed or Chaos?* (New York: Harcourt, Brace and Co, 1949), pp. 20–24.

was sustaining the life of the Universe, and as Son He was in constant union with the Father.' That is what this song *means*.

The great 5th-century Christian writer, Augustine of Hippo spoke of this breathtaking mystery like this: 'He emptied himself, taking the form of a servant, not losing the form of God. The form of a servant was *added*; the form of God did *not* pass away.' Elsewhere he writes: 'He lies in a manger, but contains the world. He feeds at the breast, but also feeds the angels. He is wrapped in swaddling clothes, but vests us with immortality. He found no place in the inn, but makes for Himself a temple in the hearts of believers. In order that weakness might become strong, strength became weak.'

The same thought was expressed in the 16th century by John Calvin, 'Even if the Word in his immeasurable essence united with the nature of man into one person, we do not imagine that he was confined therein. Here is something marvellous: the Son of God descended from heaven in such a way that, without leaving heaven, he willed to be borne in the virgin's womb, to go about the earth, and to hang upon the cross; yet he continuously filled the world even as he had done from the beginning.'

This is what it means in part to be 'made in human likeness'.

The divine death
If the song had ended there it would be more than enough to stop us in our tracks and cause us to bow down in utter wonderment before this God. What is more, it highlights the sheer emptiness of the kind of liberal theology being espoused

at the conference mentioned at the beginning of this chapter. But it doesn't end there, it goes on, '... being found in the form of a man, he humbled himself becoming obedient to death, even death on a cross.'

Some folk who are bothered about these things get a little concerned about what Paul is doing at this point because in the original language, as a hymn or poem, by adding 'even death on a cross', Paul ruins the scan. It is like the old limerick: 'There once was a poet from Japan whose poems could not possibly scan. When told this was so, he replied, "Yes, I know; that is because I always try to squeeze as many words into the last line as I possibly can."'[6] However, Paul's primary concern is not with the niceties of literature but with the wonder of the Gospel. It is the cross which forms not only the centre point of this song, but the centre point of the Christian faith. Paul is more than happy to ruin the scanning in order to get this mind-shattering, heart-rending truth over to us. And so he adds the phrase, 'even death on a cross' like an exclamation mark-scrawling the obscenity on the wall, as if to say, 'Do you really want to know how humble God is and how much he really loves us and the lengths to which he is willing to go in order to save us? I will show you: he goes to a cross!'

In his coming, God the Son became a slave, in his death he became a curse. In the one he descended to earth, in the other he descended to hell. Here is the heart of God's mission

---

6. Cited by D.A. Carson in D.A. Carson, *Basics For Believer: An Exposition of Philippians* (Baker Academic, 1996), p. 43.

foretold by Isaiah (52:13 and 53) to bear away the guilt of
sinners by absorbing into his pure and sinless body the divine
wrath we deserve because of our impure and sinful acts.
This is the divine rescue which plumbs the depths of divine
humility, as stripped naked, bruised and bleeding, his shame
is displayed before the whole watching world. God's own Son
is splayed on a cross and left to die. Christians worship the
sin-bearing God and no other religion on earth does that.

Of course, such a view of our need and God's provision
runs counter to the views many hold both within and
outside the church. If there is any sense of need at all, the
predominant belief is that we have the resources within
ourselves to meet those needs if only we knew it.

This is the religion of the Wizard of Oz.

We all know the story. Dorothy the little girl from Kansas
finds herself surrounded by brainless, heartless, spineless
people in the persons of the scarecrow, the tin man and the
lion. When Dorothy gets to the Emerald City, the Wizard
says to her what many people think God says to us. Each of
the characters comes to the Wizard with a need. Dorothy
seeks a way home. The scarecrow wants wisdom, the tin
man compassion, and the lion courage. The Wizard of Oz,
they hear, can grant all four. So they come into his presence
shivering and trembling and present their requests. His
response? He will help only *after* they demonstrate their
worthiness. 'Bring me the witch's broom' he says 'and then
I will help you.' So they do. They scale the castle walls and
destroy the witch and in the process they discover some

remarkable things about themselves. They discover they can overcome evil and do it all without the help of the Wizard. Which is a good job because when they get back to Oz they discover the Wizard isn't a Wizard after all, just some huckster—a so called 'professor'—who can put on a good performance but not help them with their problems. But the Professor redeems himself by what he shows this band of pilgrims. He tells them that they already have all that they need if only they realised it. After all didn't the scarecrow display wisdom, the tin man compassion and the lion bravery in the way they dealt with the witch? Dorothy doesn't need the help of Oz Almighty; she just needs a hot air balloon. Then Dorothy wakes up to find it was all a bad dream, her 'somewhere over the rainbow' home was right where it had always been.

The moral of the Wizard of Oz is that everything you need you already have. If you look down deep long enough and hard enough there is nothing you can't do. There it is in the popular saying; 'God helps those who help themselves.' It is the idea that God started it and we must finish it. As we saw in the first chapter, this is the religion captured in Joel Osteen's book, *Your Best Life Now*.

The lesson of Philippians 2 is strikingly different. In Christ, our salvation is an act of God from beginning to end and leaves no room for smug self-satisfaction in self-achievement.

Dr Michael Reeves in, *Christ our Life*, contrasts the Adam who was called 'son of God' with Jesus, 'Son of God' as follows,

Adam sought knowledge from the tree, and died; Christ died on his tree and won for us a knowledge altogether more wonderful; the knowledge of God. In other words, on the cross we are given not only the sweet *salvation* of God but the counterintuitive *revelation* of God. On the cross we see how humble, how self-giving, how perfectly generous and compassionate the living God is.[7]

But what does this actually mean? How are we to see *that* death which took place so long ago dealing with our sins today?

An insight might be gleaned from what happened to a Christian writer who, while visiting Jerusalem, found that one night he couldn't sleep. This is how he relates what happened next:

Towards dawn I wandered to the edge of the balconied roof and looked at the nearly empty street below. It was not entirely empty because half-way along it was a donkey pulling a dustbin into which was being loaded all the refuse from the previous day. The street where the donkey had not yet reached was full of the rubbish of yesterday, where the donkey with the dustbin had passed, everything was clean and clear ready for the new day. A donkey with a dustbin: it makes you think of the foolishness of the cross and the abasement of the one who

---

7. Michael Reeves, *Christ our Life* (Paternoster, 2014), p. 49.

walked that same road on the same kind of enterprise. 'Behold the Lamb of God who takes away the rubbish of the world.'[8]

At this point it might be worth asking yourself the question: 'Do I know the reality of Christ taking away all *my* moral mess? Are there things in my conscience which trouble me, guilty memories which haunt me?' Deep down you know that there is a God but he is little more than a 'name' flitting around your head. If God means anything to you at all, it may be that you feel he couldn't possibly be interested in someone like you, you feel too insignificant or too bad. If that is the case, then go in your mind's eye to a hill bearing three wooden crosses and ponder the one hanging in the middle. For whatever weighs you down with guilt, whatever you feel is acting as an impenetrable barrier between you and the One who made you and loves you; it has been dealt with there once and for all. You may not be able to understand the 'how', (who can fully?), but you can embrace the fact—it is done (John 19:30). Too many Christians are carrying a weight of guilt and shame they need not bear because for whatever reason they cannot or will not believe that Jesus will take it from them at Calvary. This song encourages to take it there without delay.

The divine exaltation

But how will we ever know that the sacrifice has been accepted and will be effective? We can know because of the last stanza of the song: 'Therefore, God has highly exalted him

---

8. T. Smail quoted in D. Tidball, *The Message of The Cross* (InterVarsity Press, 2001), p. 180.

and bestowed upon him the name which is above every name, that at the name of Jesus every knee should bow, in heaven, on earth and under the earth, and every tongue confess that Jesus Christ is Lord, to the glory of God the Father.'

Proof of who Jesus is and what he has done is laid out for us by his resurrection and ascension into heaven. The 'name' which now belongs to Jesus, (and which has always belonged to Jesus but has now unmistakably been made known by his exaltation), is the name 'Yahweh'/I AM—LORD.[9] Behind this verse is one of the greatest monotheistic passages of the Old Testament, Isaiah 45:23. In the Greek translation of the Old Testament (LXX) it reads, (this is Yahweh-the LORD speaking-v18), 'By myself I swear, righteousness shall go out from my mouth, my words will not be frustrated: that to me every knee shall bow and every tongue confess to God'. Back in Old Testament prophecy the LORD says there will come a time when everyone will confess him to be who he is—Saving

---

9. 'There can be no doubt that 'the name that is above every other name' (v. 9) is YHWH: it is inconceivable that any Jewish writer could use this phrase for a name other than God's own unique name. Contrary to much comment on this passage, the name itself is not 'Lord' (*kurios*: v.11), which is not the divine name nor even a Greek translation of the name, but a conventional reverential substitute for the name. However, the fact that it was a substitute for the Tetragrammaton is certainly relevant to the meaning of the passage. It connects the unique identity of God (YHWH) closely with his sovereignty (*Kurios*) as a key identifying characteristic of his uniqueness. Jesus is given the divine name because he participates in the divine sovereignty. Thus, the confession 'that Jesus Christ is Lord' (v.11) is both a surrogate for calling on him by his name, YHWH, and also a confession of his lordship.' Richard Bauckham in *Jesus and the God of Israel: God Crucified and Other Studies on the New Testament's Christology of Divine Identity* (Paternoster Press, 2008), p. 200.

Ruler. That confession will be made to 'God'. So even here you have two divine subjects in the one God, the 'LORD' who is speaking and 'God' before whom the confession will be made, (another pointer to the fact that the real God is Triune). Paul clarifies this by saying, that the LORD is Jesus and that 'God' is the Father—v. 11.[10]

We need to pause in order to consider some of the implications of this.

The passage entails the conclusion that the one who spoke to Moses from the burning bush in Exodus 3 and revealed his name to be LORD/Yahweh, 1,500 years later was to be laid in a cattle trough as the baby Jesus. It means that the one whom Isaiah saw in the Temple, 'high and lifted up' with the hem of his garment filling the whole edifice and from whom the cherubim hid their faces and cried, 'Holy, Holy. Holy is the LORD God Almighty', was 700 years later to be strung up on a Roman gibbet, left to hang on a butcher's hook like a lump of raw meat.[11] The glory he has always had, but which for a

---

10. It would be a mistake to think that the exaltation of Christ to the name above all other names indicates that prior to this he had an inferior status in his pre-incarnate state, as Bauckham rightly comments, ... the words '*ho Theos auton huperupsōsen*' (God has highly exalted him' (Philippians 2.9) ... the verb does not indicate that God has exalted Jesus to a higher status than he had previously occupied (whether in pre-existence or in mortal life), but that God has exalted him to a higher status than that of anyone or anything else, i.e. to the pre-eminent position above the whole cosmos.', Richard Bauckham in, *Jesus and the God of Israel: God Crucified and Other Studies on the New Testament's Christology of Divine Identity* (Paternoster Press, 2008), p. 208.

11. This was certainly the identification made by John in his Gospel, 'Isaiah said this because he saw Jesus' glory and spoke about him' (John. 12:41) a statement

time was hidden, is now pulsating from one end of heaven to the other and the angels cry, 'Worthy, worthy is the Lamb that was slain.' (Revelation 5:12). The whole universe bows the knee in utter devotion.

However, it would be a mistake to so emphasise the divinity of Jesus at this point that we neglect his humanity. In ascending back to the Father he did not shed his human flesh as a butterfly might shed its chrysalis. The person of the Son of God is forever united to our human nature.

This has great significance for us.

It means that there is now a human being on the throne of the universe. In the place of supreme and central significance of all creation there is a man, a member of, and the representative head of, the human race. This was what God had intended all along as we see laid out in Psalm 8 for example, where the divine mandate of Genesis 1:28 for humans to lovingly rule over God's creation is recast in poetic form (and now fulfilled in Jesus according to the writer to the Hebrews—Hebrews 2:5–9). If we were to go to the place where angels bow who never fell we would now find a man. At the very centre of the manifestation of the invisible God there is a man whose true human nature mediates the pulsating glory of God into all eternity, so that all the angels and all the creatures fall on their faces in worship and cry 'Glory'! (Revelation 5)

---

made immediately after a reference to Isaiah's commission in Isaiah 6 (John. 12:37–40).

It is little wonder that the writer to the Hebrews links the incarnation, crucifixion and ascension together, leading to the comforting truth that in Jesus we have a God who is able to assist his followers in their trials (Hebrews 2:14–18). This is another implication of the truths presented to us in the great song of Philippians 2.

Someone who found this to be true in her own experience was Rita Armstrong. For many years Rita suffered from severe depression, the bombing she experienced during the Second World War was particularly traumatic and on the whole she had a very difficult life. But she records something that happened to her one day and this is what she wrote,

> One afternoon I sat in a rare moment of peace meditating on God's greatness and power. I thought back to the blitz, then scanned through the centuries to Calvary, and back still further to the beginning of everything. And only God was there. Then I contemplated the future, the time when my life would come to an end, and forward to the day everything would be wound up. And God was still there. I felt very insignificant against such a backcloth and my petty problems paled pathetically. Then I remembered the childlike faith with which I had given my life to God, confident that Jesus loved me. And Jesus cannot change; He is the same yesterday, today and forever. Suddenly a light shone. Realisation dawned and a great joy overwhelmed me. I started to sing over and over again, 'I matter to God.'[12]

This song is meant to move us to worship Jesus. There is no

---

12. In, *Finding God in the Darkness*, ed. Irene Howat (Christian Focus, 1998).

doubt about that. But it is also meant to do something else, namely, to stir within us the desire to become more *like* Jesus, which, Paul tells us, is precisely the reason why he relates the hymn in the first place—v. 1,

> If you have any encouragement from being united with Christ, if any comfort from his love, if any fellowship (partnership) with the Spirit, if any tenderness and compassion, then make my joy complete by being like-minded, having the same love, being one in spirit and purpose. Do nothing out of selfish ambition or vain conceit, but in humility consider others better than yourselves. Each of you should look not only to your own interests, but also to the interests of others. Your attitude should be the same as that of Christ Jesus.

There then follows this great hymn. Afterwards we have the injunction, '*Therefore,* my dear friends, as you have always obeyed—not only in my presence, but now much more in my absence … do everything without grumbling or arguing, so that you may become blameless and pure …' In other words, 'follow the example of Christ I have just given you.'

Do you not find this description of the Lord Jesus to be entrancingly beautiful? Are we not forced not only to exclaim 'What a God!' but 'What a Man!'? Wouldn't it be wonderful if each one of us could be like this?

Drawing on this passage in Philippians 2, one writer puts the challenge in these terms:

The Christ whom we are trying to follow and trying to emulate made himself nothing. He became a nonentity. It was not what he was, but it was what he looked like, what he allowed men to think of him and how he allowed men to treat him. He obscured his deity beneath his humanness and ordinariness and suffering and even death. He didn't look great or clever. He had none of the trappings of popularity. Instead, he was despised and contemptible: a non-person. That is a hard road. But for the Christian it is the only road: one on which we are willing to renounce our rights, to be misunderstood, to be damned with faint praise, to serve and yet be deemed absurd failures by those we are trying to help.[13]

Christians are to worship and follow the crucified God.

---

13. Donald Macleod, *From Glory to Golgotha* (Christian Focus Publications, 2002), p. 157.

5

When God enters a Life

The work of the Holy Spirit, John 14:1–31

Imagine for a moment that I want to learn to dance. At present I can't. I might just about manage a barn dance under the careful instruction of a Caller, but when it comes to waltzes, foxtrots, salsas and the like, I am not exactly Fred Astaire! No 'Strictly Come Dancing' for me! But supposing that I decide I want to learn. In that case, being the rational, cerebral type I would go to the local bookshop and purchase—'*Dancing for Dummies*'. After all, I reason, I read a similar book to help me operate my computer in the study, so why not a book to help me operate my feet on the dance floor?

I then take the book home with me and in the quiet of my study I set to work. I do everything it says. The book says sway; I sway. The book says shuffle; I shuffle. The book says turn; I turn. I even photocopy the steps from the book and make shoe patterns which I place on the floor so I can get the steps just right.

This goes on for several weeks. Of course, during all of this time my wife is kept totally in the dark because I want to surprise her with my new-found skill. Then, when I feel confident enough, I invite her to come in and watch. I hold the book open and follow the instructions step by step. I even read the words aloud so she will be pretty impressed knowing I have done my homework. 'Lean with your right shoulder,' so I lean. 'Now step with your right foot,' so I step. 'Turn slowly to the left,' so I turn.

I continue to read, then dance, then read, then dance until the dance is finally over and I collapsed exhausted in the chair. I then look at Heather, my wife and I exclaim—'There! What do you think of that? I executed the dance perfectly.' She looks back at me, shaking her head in pity. 'You certainly did execute it' she says, 'you killed it!' 'What do you mean?' I reply. 'Well, you forgot the most important part—the music.' I had not even given a thought to the music. I had bought the book, learnt the rules, laid out the pattern but forgot all about the music. Not only that, but I would have done better having a dancing partner! So my wife gets up, she puts on the CD, takes my hand and—off we go. Before I know where I am, I am dancing, *really* dancing and I don't even have the book![1]

---

1. I owe this illustration to Max Lucado, 'Music for the Dance' in *His Voice*, (Word, 1991).

What is the point of that little parable?

It is this.

Sometimes Christians can be so tight on following the book that they forget the music. That is, we might know our Bibles backwards, perhaps having been brought up on the stories of Jesus, fascinated by the deeds of David, and even managed to get some key doctrines under our belt. We then set out on the dance floor of the Christian life with the book but with no music in our hearts and no animation in our souls. We, as it were, measure each step, note each turn and then finish the day exhausted because we have danced only with the book in our own strength. Dancing with no music and just a book is hardly going to be a joy. Also, not to have a partner who would be with us in the dance of life is hardly dancing at all. And yet, it is possible to own the name of Christ merely following rules without a relationship. Christ's commands are vital, as we shall see, in fact without them there is no Christian life to be had, but they are given to enhance the personal relationship with him and are not meant to be a substitute for it.

On the night before his death when the disciples were beginning to get anxious with all this talk about him 'going away' Jesus introduced them to the great music maker of the Trinity—the Holy Spirit. We read all about it in John 14.

The person of the Holy Spirit

As Jesus gathers his remaining disciples around him on that fateful night, he has been driving home the disturbing truth that he is going to be leaving them by way of the cross (John 13). And just when all seems lost and bleak (the disciple's hearts were 'troubled' John 14:1), he makes a wonderful promise which is linked to a condition, v. 15: 'If you love me, you will obey what I command. And I will ask the Father, and he will give you another Counsellor to be with you forever—the Spirit of truth.'

Many Christians if asked to describe God as their heavenly Father would probably be able to do so. They might speak of him as the Creator who has made us and cares for us. Similarly, if asked to say something of God the Son, they would no doubt be able to make a decent job of it, perhaps speaking of him as the second person of the Trinity, 'the incarnate Word', who came to die on the cross for our sins and, having been raised to life as the rightful ruler of the world, will one day return to wind up history. This is the stuff of the Nicene Creed. But if asked to describe the Holy Spirit and his work, more often than not that might be met with an embarrassing silence. Of the three persons of the Godhead, the Holy Spirit is the one we seem to understand the least. The Holy Spirit seems a shadowy figure, and even more so when he used to be referred to as the 'Holy Ghost'! Perhaps the most common mistake is to think of the Holy Spirit as being more of a power than a person. Even within Pentecostalism and the Charismatic movement this is the predominant way of thinking and speaking—as if the Spirit were some sort of liquid to fill us up or a gas to blow us away. Such is not the understanding the Lord Jesus gives here.

That the Holy Spirit is a person is made clear in verse 17

when Jesus says, 'The world cannot accept *him*, because it neither sees *him* nor knows *him*. But you know *him*, for *he* lives with you and will be in you.' Verse 16 unpacks for us the *kind* of person he is: 'I will ask the Father, and he will give you *another Counsellor* to be with you forever-—the Spirit of truth.' Jesus is promising to send 'another Counsellor'. There are two words in the original language which can be translated 'another'. It could be 'another type altogether'—a *different kind* of counsellor. Or it could be 'another of the same kind'.[2] That is what is meant here. But what kind of 'another'? The answer: another like the one who is speaking—Jesus. Jesus is going back to heaven via the cross and he will then ask his Father to send someone just like himself.[3]

So what is Jesus doing by describing this other person who will come from the Father and the Son, that is, from heaven where they rule, as a 'Counsellor'? It may seem to us a rather odd word to use. Strictly translated it is *'paraklētos'*—meaning 'someone called alongside to assist', 'to encourage' or 'to exhort'. In secular Greek it referred to someone who was called to assist in court—a legal assistant. Thus the term 'Counsellor' would be more associated with the American legal system of having 'counsel' rather than the English

---

2. '*allon paraklēton*'.

3. In 16:13, John breaks all the rules of Greek Grammar by using a personal pronoun with a neuter subject (Spirit—to talk of the Spirit as 'he' rather than 'it'.) 'But when he, the Spirit of truth, comes, he will guide you into all truth. He will not speak on his own; he will speak only what he hears, and he will tell you what is yet to come.' He is as personal as God the Father and God the Son, and just as we wouldn't think of referring to either Father or Son as 'it', neither should we the Spirit. Also, as Father and Son are persons and equally divine, so is the Holy Spirit.

notion of a family counsellor.[4] Some Bible translations render the word 'Comforter' which is certainly one way of thinking about the Spirit, not particularly in wiping away tears, but in the old English sense of the word as someone who strengthens.

All these ideas come together in terms of an assisting, strengthening role. This is what Jesus himself has been doing with his disciples while physically on earth, which is now about to end. It is what he is supremely doing now during these last few hours together. And so the Paraclete that he and the Father are about to send will continue to do more of the same; 'John 14 implies that during *his earthly ministry* his role as Paraclete, strengthening and helping his disciples, was discharged on earth. "Another Paraclete" is given to perform this latter task.'[5]

It is also important to note the close and intimate relationship between the Father, Son and Spirit in this passage, in particular, how they 'indwell' each other.

In John 14:10–11 we read: 'Don't you believe that I am in the Father, and that the Father is in me? The words I say to you are not just my own. Rather, it is the Father, living in me, who is doing his work. Believe me when I say that I am in the Father and the Father is in me.'

---

4. It is in John 16:7–11 that the legal overtones of the work of the Spirit are the most striking. But this is in terms of a prosecuting attorney rather than someone employed for the defence.

5. D. A. Carson, *The Gospel According to John* (InterVarsity Press, 1991), p. 500.

This reveals the special and intimate nature of the relationship between the Father and the Son such that to encounter the one is to simultaneously encounter the other. If you are in the presence of the Son you are also in the presence of the Father for the Son mediates his presence. This means that we are not to think of Father and Son as two individuals who have an existence independent of each other. Rather, their identity (who they are) arises out of their relationship to each other. God the Father is Father by virtue of the fact that he has an eternally begotten Son. The Son is Son by virtue of the fact that he is eternally begotten of the Father. Yet they remain distinct persons, for you need at least two 'centres of consciousness' to love—a lover and a beloved.[6]

The writer Tom Smail describes the relationship in this way: 'The "fellowship of the Holy Spirit" (2 Corinthians 13:14) revealed in God's relating to us reflects that "fellowship" within the life of God ... The Spirit can be seen as the person who mediates, sustains and enables the love between the Father and the Son, so that by his personal action he both unites them in an inexpressibly close way but at the same time constitutes himself as "the space" between them so that they do not collapse into each other but remain in their

---

6. This mutual indwelling which ensures the unity of the Godhead whilst still respecting the distinctiveness of persons, has been given a name by the Eastern Church theologians (which goes back to John of Damascus in the 8th century), it is called 'perichoresis'. The theologian Miroslav Volf describes it as 'co-inherence in one another without any coalescence or commixture.' Miroslav Volf, *After Our Likeness: The Church as the Image of the Trinity* (Grand Rapids, MI: Eerdmans, 1998), p. 209.

distinct personal integrity over against each other.' He goes
on to write,

> This is what we see happening in the baptism of Jesus, where
> the Father gives himself to the Son in giving him his Spirit
> and remains distinct from the incarnate Son in his heavenly
> glory. He is thus the Spirit who, by simultaneously relating and
> maintaining the distinct personhood of the other two, is not
> reduced to a relationship but is to be seen as the person who
> completes and unites the godhead in his relating of the Father
> to the Son.[7]

That is a wonderful picture, which resonates much with
what C. S. Lewis called 'the great dance'.

The purpose of the Holy Spirit
This brings us to the role of the Spirit in the lives of Christ's
followers.

He is someone who is constantly with the follower of Jesus,
v. 15 he will 'be with you forever' and v. 17, 'you know him for
he lives *with* you and will be *in* you.'

I still have very vivid memories of my Dad teaching me to
ride my bike when I was about 5 years old. He took me to the
back of our terraced house, which was really a mud track, and
rather gingerly I would get onto the bike with my knuckles
white from gripping the handle bars too tight. He would push

---

7. Tom Smail, *Like Father, Like Son: The Trinity Imaged in our Humanity*
(Paternoster, 2005), p.100.

me along, holding on to the saddle and urge me to peddle, telling me to keep my eyes fixed straight ahead. All the while as I peddled I would call out, 'Are you still there?' He would reassure me he was, then he would let go, I would panic and fall off. I would get back on the saddle and try again. The moment came when I was peddling away furiously, still anxiously asking, 'Dad are you there?', that I found myself cycling and heard my Dad laughing about fifty feet down the road. I was actually cycling by myself!

According to Jesus, the Holy Spirit both *is* and is *not* like my Dad. He is like him in that he is someone who comes alongside to assist the Christian, as my Dad was beside or behind me helping me keep my balance. This is not all that bad a way of thinking about his role as 'Helper' for he helps the Christian to keep his balance as it were. But one major difference is this, whereas my Dad left me once I had got going myself, the Holy Spirit doesn't leave us. This spatial imagery of being 'with' us preserves the Holy Spirit's distinctiveness as a person.

But even more startling is the preposition Jesus uses, that the Comforter will be 'in' us. In this way he works differently to the way Jesus did while he was on earth. Then Jesus was 'with' his disciples, but not 'in' them. Here we are told the Spirit will be 'in' all the followers of Jesus for all time. So why is he with us and in us? Jesus goes on to explain.

In the first instance the Spirit *mediates the presence of Jesus*, verse 18: 'I will not leave you as orphans; *I* will come to you.' Jesus has just been speaking about sending the

Helper, the Holy Spirit to be with and in his followers and he immediately follows this up by speaking of *himself* being with them. But how can he when he has already told them he is going away back to the Father? It is because once he goes back to heaven God's presence amongst his people will be mediated by God the Holy Spirit.

Also the Holy Spirit *unites us with God*, v. 20 'On that day (the day of the giving of the Holy Spirit at Pentecost) you will realise that I am in my Father and you are in me and I am in you.' There is this spiritual unity between Christian believers and God, a unity like that within the Trinity itself. You cannot get a more intimate relationship than that!

But there is more—v. 23b, 'My Father will love him, and we will come to him and make our home with him.' This is astonishing! Jesus is claiming that the Holy Spirit's function is to mediate the presence of *both* the Father and the Son, ensuring a Trinitarian presence in the life of a believer. The Spirit is equal to the Father and the Son as God. But as the Father's role is to love the Son and honour him by giving all glory to him, and the Son's role is to love and obey the Father and so honour him—including obeying the Father's will to go to the cross (John 17:1), one of the Spirit's roles is to bring the Father and the Son into the hearts and lives of Christian believers, making their 'home' there.[8]

---

8. In verse 2 Jesus speaks of there being many 'abodes' (*monai*) in his Father's 'house' which already exist for his followers. But Jesus provides access to a place (*topon*) for his followers by way of the cross (this is the preparation of which he speaks in verse 3). In verse 23 Jesus speaks of him and his Father taking up residence (*monen*) within his followers.

As he lives in us and brings God to us, what does he do? Verse 25–27: 'All this I have spoken while still with you. But the Counsellor, the Holy Spirit, whom the Father will send in my name, will teach you all things and will remind you of everything I have said to you. Peace I leave with you; my peace I give you. I do not give to you as the world gives. Do not let your hearts be troubled and do not be afraid.'

Think again of Jesus. What did he do with his followers? Primarily he taught them the Gospel, the truth about God. More than that in his own person he embodied that truth, displaying in the rough and tumble of life what God was really like—a lover of holiness, full of compassion and mercy, being a kindly ruler. He also came to show us what it was to live a true human life, one which happily submits to God and his ways, as one who serves. That is what *this* Helper will do, who is described as the Spirit of Truth.

In the first instance with these 11 disciples (Judas has left by now to betray Jesus—John. 13:30) Jesus promises that the Holy Spirit will 'teach you all things and remind you of everything I said to you.'(v. 26) That is why we can trust the New Testament which his followers wrote. The Holy Spirit of Truth inspired them so that they remembered infallibly the words of Jesus and all he did.[9] And so since God the Spirit inspired them, what the Bible says is what God says. The

---

9. In John. 16:12, Jesus reinforces this role of the Spirit, 'I have much more to say to you, more than you can now bear. But when he, the Spirit of truth, comes, he will guide you into all the truth. He will not speak on his own; he will speak only what he hears, and he will tell you what is yet to come. He will glorify me because it is from me that he will receive what he will make known to you. All that

Book, the Bible *is* important, for this is where we hear the words of God and discover Jesus. However, in a secondary sense *all* Christians are taught by the Holy Spirit—not apart from the words he inspired the apostles to write but *through* them. Going back to our original picture he enables us to hear the music and not just read the book—so by the Spirit the Bible becomes a wonderful book, alive, full of life and light.

What is more, as we read the promises of Christ that he will not leave us as orphans but come to dwell within us by his Spirit, we then receive his peace. No one wants to be left alone by bereavement. No child wants to become an orphan (v. 18), no one wants to become a widow, and the disciples don't want to be left alone without Jesus. Why, things were difficult enough while he was with them with all that opposition and misunderstanding—what hope would they have of getting things right once he had gone? But Jesus tries to allay their fears by saying he will come again, but his presence will be in the form of the Holy Spirit. This promise which is fulfilled by the Holy Spirit produces peace, the quiet knowledge that Jesus has kept his Word—he *is* with us.

Since the Helper is inside the believer we are given something else—a new power. Sometimes people think that being a Christian is just a matter of following routine, treating the Bible as a book of rules, a set of 'dos and don'ts'. The book is vital as we have seen, this is where we meet God and discover how we should live. This is where we find the

---

belongs to the Father is mine. That is why I said the Spirit will receive from me what he will make known to you.'

promises which give us peace. But you not only need to know how to dance, but have the *ability* to dance and more than that have a partner to dance with. The Holy Spirit fulfils both roles. He is the one who ultimately wrote the book—how to 'dance' or live the Christian life, and so with him living in us he gives us power to start living it out.

But it is also a matter of developing a relationship with him, allowing him to be the leading partner, like a partner who takes the lead in a dance. Or to change the picture very slightly, Paul in his letter to the Galatians urges us to 'keep in step' with the Spirit. To love the things he loves and hate the things he hates. What are those? Read the Bible and you will find out.

The role of the Holy Spirit working *within* the life of a believer and bringing glory to Christ (John 16:14) goes some way towards explaining why the Holy Spirit does appear to be rather vague in our thinking. This is how C. S. Lewis describes the role of the Holy Spirit in the life of the believer:

> In the Christian life you are not usually looking *at* Him. He is always acting through you. If you think of the Father as something 'out there', in front of you, and of the Son as someone standing at your side, helping you to pray, trying to turn you into another son, then you have to think of the third Person as something inside you or behind you. Perhaps some people find it easier to begin with the third person and work backwards. God is love, and that love works through men— especially the whole community of Christians. But this spirit of love is, from all eternity, a love going on between the Father

and the Son ... The whole dance, or drama, or pattern of this
three-Personal life is to be played out in each one of us; or
(putting it the other way round) each one of us has got to enter
that pattern, take his place in that dance. There is no other way
to the happiness for which we were made.'[10]

The prerequisite of the Holy Spirit

There is, however, a prerequisite or precondition for us
knowing these things in experience which up to this point
we have passed over, 'If you love me you will *obey* what
I command and I will ask the father to send you another
Counsellor.'[11] Later in v. 23 this is reiterated, 'If anyone loves
me, he will *obey* my teaching—and the Father will love him
and we will come and make our home with him.'

If children love their parents they will show that love and
respect by doing what they are told. If a husband loves his
wife he will do what his wife asks of him, if it is for her good
and the good of the family. So it is with us and God.

We first receive the Holy Spirit by obeying the teaching of
Jesus, that is, by believing the Gospel promise that 'whoever
believes on him should not perish but have everlasting life'.
This is how we become disciples. What is more, we continue
to be a follower by doing what he says. Remember the Holy
Spirit is a person. That means, according to the Bible, we can

---

10. C. S. Lewis, *Mere Christianity* (Harper-Collins, 2001), p. 176.

11. 'Barrett rightly observes that the protasis, *"If you love* me" controls the
grammar of the next two verses (15–17a), and the thought of the next six' (15–21).
D. A. Carson, in D. A. Carson, *The Gospel According to John* (Inter Varsity Press,
1991), p. 498.

grieve him, disobey him, and even, in the case of Ananias and Sapphira, lie to him and look at what happened to them—they died on the spot! (Acts 5:1-11). If the dance is going to be a smooth one, then *both* partners need to keep in time and follow the same steps. The Holy Spirit gently leads us in that dance, comforting, encouraging, correcting, and strengthening. He will not lead us to do something opposed to what he has written down in the Bible, but always encouraging us to obey what is written. The music he wants to bring into our hearts is the music of heaven, the great song of the great dance which we read about in the Book of Revelation. What is that? It is the song which puts Jesus where he rightly ought to be on the throne at the centre of the Universe as he should be at the centre of out lives: 'To him who sits on the throne and to the Lamb be praise and honour and glory and power for ever and ever.' (Revelation 5:13).

A little later on Jesus is going warn his disciples of the opposition they will face (John 15:18-25). In such circumstances the followers of Jesus must testify to him, and it will be the Counsellor who will help them do that (John 15:26-27). And so we might ask, whether all this talk of 'dance' is rather frivolous?

Later in chapter 17 Jesus prays for his disciples, v. 13, 'I am coming to you now, but I say these things while I am still in the world, so that they may have the full measure of my joy within them.' Just prior to that, he is concerned that his troubled followers would know joy, 15:11, 'These things I have spoken to you, that my joy may be in you, and that your joy may be full.' It would appear that Jesus is saying that in the midst of difficulty and opposition, his disciples can know joy. How will that joy be communicated? The answer is by this other Paraclete. After all, it was the Holy Spirit who enabled Jesus to experience joy, 'At that time Jesus, full of joy through the Holy Spirit, said "I praise you Father, the Lord of heaven and earth, because you have hidden these things from the wise and learned, and revealed them to little children. Yes, Father, for this is what you were pleased to do."' (Luke 10:21).

And so the picture of the strengthening, sustaining, work of the Spirit, who brings into the lives of the believer the Triune God, as one who leads us in a joyous dance even in the midst of difficulty, is not so strange after all. This was understood by C. S. Lewis who captured this wonderful reality in story form.

One of the greatest characters of all children's literature must be Aslan—the great Lion King of Narnia, who is the Christ-like figure in the stories. In the book, *Prince Caspian*, Lewis depicts the joy that can be had with Christ even in the midst of a mighty battle by having Aslan organise a grand parade and party:

> Everyone was awake, everyone was laughing, flutes were playing, cymbals clashing … 'What is it, Aslan?' said Lucy, for her eyes were dancing and her feet wanting to dance. 'Come children,' said he. 'Ride on my back again today.' 'Oh lovely!' cried Lucy and both girls climbed onto the warm golden back. Then the whole party moved off—Aslan leading, Bacchus and

his Maenads leaping, rushing and turning somersaults and the beasts frisking around them.[12]

I don't think that it was simply to appeal to children that Lewis cast the main characters in his stories as children. May it not be in part that it is especially children that are most God-like in this respect. They know what it is to have uninhibited joy. Aslan elicits joy, a song, a dance. The Counsellor imparts that joy and life to the believer.

---

12. C.S Lewis, *Prince Caspian* (Fontana, 1982), p. 169.

6

When God is Proclaimed

The necessity of Gospel proclamation, Romans 10:12–18

Boris Nikolayevich Kornfeld was a medical doctor, a Jew who grew up in post-revolutionary Russia. Given the vicious anti-Semitism promoted by successive Tsars, what was being offered by this new socialism would have seemed far more attractive to his parents than anything the Jews could have hoped for under so-called, 'Christian' Russia. Maybe atheistic Russia would save them?

Whatever hopes they may have had were soon to be dashed by the purges of Josef Vissarionovich, better known as Josef Stalin, which means 'steel', a name given by his contemporaries who fell under his steel-like will. The persecutions in Russia remained the same; it was simply the persecutors' names which had changed. And so it was that Dr

Kornfeld found himself imprisoned in a concentration camp reserved for political subversives—Ekibastuz.

It was in this hell on earth that Kornfeld began to re-evaluate his previous beliefs. It was here of all places, that Kornfeld did something which would have horrified his forebears: he became a Christian.[1]

We have been seeing how nothing less than a deep, Trinitarian belief in God will topple the idols of today and ensure a healthy, robust Christian life. In this chapter we consider what is necessary for anyone to come to know this God at all and so displace whatever god-substitutes they may have, indeed, what was necessary for Kornfeld to become a believer

This was a question which occupied the mind of the apostle Paul in one of his greatest letters, his epistle to the Romans. It is in chapter 10 that he particularly wrestles with this issue.

The bad news before the good news

In the first three chapters of this letter Paul has been painting a very bleak picture of the human race. He has shown how despite God's general revelation of himself, including the *sensus divinitatis*—the sense of the divine we all have deep within, our natural tendency is towards idolatry; 'they exchanged the glory of the immortal God for images.' (Romans 1:23). What is more, in an act of judgement, God gives people over to the pride and desires of their own

---

1. Charles Colson, *Loving God* (Zondervan 1983), pp. 27–34.

hearts, 'Because of this God gave them over to shameful lusts'—all very much the stuff of the King of Tyre. Eventually the apostle comes to the conclusion that, in the words of G. K. Chesterton, not only are we all in the same boat, but we are all seasick! 'What shall we conclude then ...There is no one righteous, not even one' (Romans 3:10). There then follows a chain of Old Testament Scripture quotations to prove his point: the whole world stands condemned. The sickness of which Paul speaks is the universal sickness of sin, the pathological spiritual virus which makes us into God's enemies and wreckers of his world.

It is against this dark backdrop of our universal need that the bright shining light of God's universal provision breaks through in the person of Jesus Christ. Having dealt with our guilt on the cross, Jesus was raised from the dead and unites us with himself, a gift received by faith. In the giving of his Spirit he provides a new life and sets us out in a new direction—heavenward, 'Therefore being justified by faith, we have peace with God through our Lord Jesus Christ: By whom also we have access by faith into this grace wherein we stand, and rejoice in hope of the glory of God. (Romans 5:1–2).

But if God has done all of this for *all* humanity where does that leave Israel—the Jews? Has God abandoned them in favour of the Gentiles, because if he has, then how can we trust him not to abandon us at some point in the future? That is the question Paul tackles in chapters 9–11.

The short answer to that question is, no, God has not

abandoned the Jews. But neither has he set up a two track system of salvation, so that Jews get saved one way (by being Jewish) and non-Jews get saved another way (by being 'Christian'). God's plan is far more wonderful than that.

One Lord with one purpose

The underlying theological basis for the unity of God's plan of redemption is underscored in v. 12, 'For there is no difference between Jew and Gentile—the same Lord is Lord of all and richly blesses all who call on him.' Here we are told quite categorically that God wants to bless, literally 'bestow riches'. This is not a God who reluctantly tosses the odd favour in our direction like a city banker might throw a coin to someone selling the *Big Issue* outside a London Underground station. He delights to give riches. And what riches! There is the blessing of sins forgiven, 'Therefore, there is no condemnation for those who are in Christ Jesus' (Romans 8:1). This is but a means to a greater end which is the gift of *royal sonship*, to be loved by God the Father, just like the Father loves Jesus—God the Son; 'For those God foreknew he also predestined to be conformed to the image of his Son, that he might be the firstborn among many brothers.' (Romans 8:30). Note too that this astonishing blessing is for '*everyone*'—all kinds of people. We can never accuse God of being mean. His character defines generosity.

But, this gift of sonship is not automatic, there is a condition. It is for 'all who *call* on him'.

One way of salvation

The issue Paul is dealing with is salvation, v. 13, for, 'Everyone who calls on the name of the Lord will be *saved*.' Christianity is not a moral self-improvement programme; it is news about a rescue from certain disaster—a judgement to come. It is freedom from a tyranny we cannot shake off now matter how hard we try.

This was something which Boris Kornfeld recognised to be his basic problem.

As a doctor in the frozen wastes of Siberia he was called upon to treat fellow prisoners. He saw many terrible sights during his imprisonment, but it was his own *self*-diagnosis which horrified him the most. He became appalled at the hatred and the violence within his own heart. Yes, *he* had been a victim of hatred and violence as his ancestors had been. But that hatred had spawned a hatred of its own. He saw his predicament, that he was trapped by the very evil he despised. What freedom could he ever know while he was in that state? He needed someone to set him free from a bondage far more lasting and far more serious than the one forced upon him in the Gulag. That is, he needed salvation.

That this has always been God's concern is underscored by the quotation from the book of Joel which Paul refers to, that 'all who call upon the name of the Lord will be saved'. This is Old Testament stuff—it's not new. Neither is it peculiar to the apostle Paul, because Peter quotes this very same verse in his first sermon on the Day of Pentecost in Acts 2. But who is the 'Lord' that people are to call upon in order to be rescued? For Joel the answer was God—Yahweh/LORD. But both Peter and Paul give a face and a name to this Lord—he is *Jesus*—that is what Paul has said in verse 9, 'Confess with your mouth that *Jesus* is Lord'.

People call on the name of the Lord for all sorts of reasons in moments of crisis. But the Lord they are calling on is often not really God; he is some celestial repair-man who is called in to fix things when we can't. But after the crisis—back he goes until the next time. Again we return to idols of the imagination.

By way of stark contrast, the 'calling' Paul and Joel are speaking of is more like the call of a man trapped in a burning building who sees no way out but who suddenly hears a sound through the thick, toxic smoke, which is the voice of a rescuer. And so he cries out, 'Help me, I'm trapped in here'.

The Bible teaches that we are in a similar fix, trapped by our sin and engulfed by lostness. But as we saw in the wonderful hymn of Philippians 2, in Jesus Christ God graciously comes down to lift us out and lift us up. There are no other rescuers around. It is *the* Lord who is to be called upon, not '*a* Lord' or '*a* God'. That Lord has a name—Jesus.

This then sets off a train of questions in Paul's mind which he pursues with unrelenting logic in vv. 14–15. If anyone is to call upon the Lord Jesus, then that means they first have to believe. But the only way they are going to believe in him is if they are told about him. And if they are to be told about him, then it follows there has to be someone who does the telling. What is more, no one is going to do the telling unless they are told to get on with the telling, that is, they have to be sent.

What is central to this chain of thinking is that salvation comes through believing a *message*. It is messages: words of promise, words of forgiveness, words which tell of an action by God which has taken place to change things—that have to be heard and so proclaimed.

One message through which people are saved

Just as there is one Lord—Jesus, and one way of salvation—believing in Jesus, then there is only one message about Jesus, vv. 16–17, 'For Isaiah says, "Lord who has believed our *message*?" Consequently faith comes from hearing *the* message and *the* message is heard through *the* word of Christ.'

This is not a novelty, something Paul has made up, it is the same message Isaiah proclaimed, in chapter 53 of his book 700 years earlier, which is where this quote comes from. It is a message which speaks of a crucified and resurrected Christ who dies for the sins of his people. Paul has already unpacked what this 'word of Christ' is in verse 9 which folk must believe in order to be saved, namely, '… if you confess with your mouth, "Jesus is Lord," and believe in your heart that God raised him from the dead, you will be *saved*.'

This tells us something very important about the nature of *saving* faith.

According to Lewis Carroll's White Queen in *Alice Through the looking Glass*, 'Faith' is believing 'six impossible things before breakfast.' If ever there was a misunderstood word today both within and outside Christian circles, it is that little word 'faith'. Part of the problem is that it is seen as something distinctly religious. The religious person has 'faith' whereas the non-religious person doesn't. 'Faith' is uncertain and takes over when certainty and facts come to an end. This is a great pity because the Bible's use of the word 'faith' (*pistis*) is not intrinsically religious at all. It is a very common word referring to something which all people are doing all of the time. Perhaps for the sake of clarity we should drop the word 'faith' altogether in our discussions on religion and substitute some of the more ordinary alternatives. The alternatives would be: 'trust', 'rely', 'depend'. There are two reasons why these words convey the real meaning better than the word 'faith'.

First, because faith isn't a thing we possess, it is something we *do*—'trusting', 'relying', 'depending'—there is no such word as 'faithing'.

Secondly, they underscore the importance of the *object* of faith, for when someone says, 'I trust', you ask, 'Trust in what'? When they say, 'I depend', you ask 'On what are you depending?' When they claim, 'I rely'—well, the sentence is incomplete. You have to finish it by saying upon what it is you are relying. But if someone simply says, 'I have faith' it appears very mystical but doesn't tell you very much.

What is more, it is the *object* of faith that makes faith rational in that you 'depend' upon something dependable, you 'rely' upon something reliable, you 'trust' something that is trustworthy. Therefore, this word 'faith' has a flip side. You must put your faith in something faithful, for to put your trust in something untrustworthy isn't faith, it is gullibility.

Having faith is a universal phenomenon. Having saving faith isn't.

It is the *object* of this faith, called saving faith (which denotes its effect), which is going to get us from this world to the next by bringing us into a personal relationship with God, which is distinct. It has three elements. If *any* one is missing, then whatever we have it is not *Christian* faith.

First, faith consists of *facts*—knowing things to be *true*. All believing has this knowledge component. If I say that I believe that a particular chair is able to support me, the first thing I have to be sure of is that there is a chair there in the first place. There is or there isn't. It is a matter of fact. This is the case with the Christian message, it has *factual* content. It concerns Jesus Christ, a historical figure, who is Lord—the same God as in the Old Testament whose name was Yahweh-LORD. This God-man Jesus was raised from the dead, which means he had died. What is more, this was a special death as it was a sacrifice for sins which turns away God's anger and makes him favourable towards us (the technical word for this is *propitiation*). Those things are either true or not true. If that is not proclaimed or believed, then there is no Gospel and so no salvation.

The second part of faith is *assent*; it is through our mouths that we express what is in our minds. Again, this is not anything specifically religious. If I am asked 'Do you believe that a particular chair can support you?' two things will be necessary for me to answer in the affirmative. First, I believe there *is* a chair. And second, I really do *think* the chair will be able to support me if I were to sit on it. I verbally 'assent' to my belief.

But it is possible to have both of these things in relation to Jesus Christ and it would *still* not make you a Christian for this very simple reason: the demons believe both of those things. In fact they believe them far more deeply than you or I ever will; 'Show me your faith without deeds, and I will show you my faith by my deeds. You believe that there is one God. Good! Even the demons believe that and shudder' (James 2:19). Of course, such belief doesn't make them into Christians!

It is both sad and dangerous when people put themselves in the same position as the devils. Yes, they believe Jesus existed. They believe he died on the cross. When presented with all the evidence, they would even be willing to say, 'Jesus rose from the dead'. And yet it does not make any perceivable difference to their lives because of the absence of the third element—*trust*. Going back to our illustration of the chair, the progression of faith is as follows: I believe there is a chair. I believe it can support me. I am going to put that belief into action by *sitting* on it. Paul describes this vital element as believing in your *'heart'*—v9. 'It is with your *heart* you believe and so are justified.'

We tend to think of the heart as the seat of the emotions. And so we speak of 'heartthrobs', or 'heartaches' and 'broken

hearts'. That is not what the Bible means by the word. For
the Hebrew it was the kidneys which were thought of as
being the location of the emotions! Rather, the heart was the
totality of the inner person, the very centre of the personality.
It was the cockpit of the soul if you will. As such it was the
origin of desires, affections, perceptions, thoughts, reasoning,
imagination, purpose, will and faith. That is the heart. The
book of Proverbs understandably admonishes us: 'Above
all else, guard your heart, for it is the well spring of life.'
(Proverbs 4:23).

Trust, then, is something deep down and volitional.
Christians are to be 'F.A.T.'—having a faith composed of
*F*acts, *A*ssent and *T*rust.

But of course we are not talking about believing in an *object*
like a chair, but believing in a *person*, someone who is so
unimaginably pure and kind, whose moral beauty is more
entrancing than the most stunning sunset and who will never
renege on his promises—especially the promise to save those
who call on him. We are talking about believing in the Lord
Jesus Christ.

This was something Kornfeld discovered in his own
experience.

In the Gulag he came into contact with a fellow inmate
who was a devout Christian. One day this man spoke to him
of a Jewish Messiah who had come to keep the promises
the Lord had made to Israel. He pointed out that Jesus had
spoken mostly to Jewish people, which was consistent with

God's special concern for the Jews, the chosen ones. He explained that through his death on the cross he atoned for sins and ushered in a new kingdom of peace. The Gulag had taken away from Kornfeld everything, including his belief of salvation through socialism. Now for the first time in years this man offered him hope.

Unexpectedly, he began to see parallels between the Jews and Jesus. It had always been a scandal that God should entrust himself in a unique way to one group of people, the Jews. Despite centuries of persecution, their very existence was a sign that there was a greater Power than that of their persecutors. It was the same with Jesus. Here was someone who appeared weak, despised and yet whose presence and words confounded the world. Jesus seemed to stand as a sign to a greater Power and was perceived as a threat only to be killed. Over time, very gradually, Kornfeld came to understand the *facts* of the Gospel. Then step by step he began to *assent* to the truth of the Gospel. Until eventually he opened his *heart* to the Gospel as he discovered Jesus to be the long promised Messiah.

This was a truth which not only changed him, but was to cost him his life.

It happened in this way.

One day while he was doing his rounds he came across one of his many patients suffering from pellagra, induced by malnutrition which in turn made digestion very difficult, resulting in its victims literally starving to death. Kornfeld had been giving the patient chalk, good bread and herring to stop the diarrhoea and to ensure that nutrients got into the blood. But the man was too far gone. Just after leaving this patient, Kornfeld came across a hulk of an orderly who was bent over, eating the remains of a loaf of white bread which was meant for the pellagra patients. He looked up shamelessly with his cheeks stuffed with food. Kornfeld had been aware of the stealing that was going on and was also conscious that this was one of the reasons why the patients weren't recovering. The reason why such orderlies were not reported was that whoever did the reporting soon wound up dead. But this time Kornfeld did what he thought was right and reported the theft to the camp commandant who was shocked, not with the stealing but with the fact that Kornfeld had effectively signed his own death warrant. Kornfeld's heart had been changed by the Gospel.

One task to fulfil

But the message which changes Kornfeld's life had to be brought to him. *Someone* told Boris Kornfeld the Gospel otherwise he would not have heard and so not have been saved. Which brings us to the final point concerning the task Christians have been given by the Triune God, vv. 14–15: 'How can they hear without someone preaching to them? And how can they proclaim unless they are sent.'

There are many things which the church does which the world can do perfectly well by itself. Society can help the physically and mentally ill. The wider society can help the poor and marginalised. Society can step in with aid to meet major disasters. Christians and Christian organisations do all of these things too—and where they can they should. But there is one thing the world will never do and that is tell people about the saving love of God in Jesus Christ. This is *the* unique task of the Church. If Christians don't do it—no one else will. This is why Jesus sent his followers into the world with the Gospel message: 'Then Jesus came to them and said, "All authority in heaven and on earth has been given to me. Therefore as you go, make disciples of all nations, baptising them into the name of the Father and of the Son and of the Holy Spirit, and teach them to obey everything I have commanded you. And surely I am with you always, to the very end of the age."' (Matthew 28:18–20)

Today it is not unusual to find firms, schools and even churches with logos. According to this passage of Paul's, a suitable logo which would symbolise quite succinctly the church's mission statement would be a pair of feet! In God's sight, those Christians who share the message of the Lord Jesus over a cup of coffee, by a hospital bedside, with that parent at the school gate or with that fellow student in the lecture theatre—have *beautiful* feet. That is what Paul says in v. 15 quoting Isaiah 52:7, 'How beautiful are the feet of those who bring good news'. Some of those feet may be worn out because they have travelled the world with this message. Others will be steady feet, determined feet—set in that singular direction of praying for an opportunity to speak to someone about Christ. The truth is we may never fully know the ultimate effect a simple conversation with a non-Christian friend might have.

This was the case with Boris Kornfeld.

One night, Kornfeld shared with a patient, who was experiencing excruciating pain due to stomach cancer, the wonderful freedom he had recently found in Christ. Part of that confession involved stating openly that he believed we *all* deserved to suffer because of the way we have behaved towards other people and God. He said, 'On the whole, you know, I have become convinced that there is no punishment that comes to us in this life on earth which is undeserved. Superficially, it can have nothing to do with what we are guilty of in actual fact, but if you go over your life with a fine-tooth comb and ponder deeply, you will always be able to hunt down that transgression of yours for which you have now received a blow.'

What the doctor said to that patient began to have an effect in *his* heart.

The young patient awoke the next morning to the sound of running feet and a commotion in the area of the operating theatre. His first thought was of the doctor, but his new friend did not come. Then the whispers of a fellow patient told him of Kornfeld's fate. During the night, while the doctor slept, someone had crept up beside him and dealt him eight blows on the head of a plasterer's mallet. And though his fellow doctors worked hard to save him, in the morning the orderlies carried him out, a still, broken form.

Kornfeld had died, but his testimony to Christ was to live on.

The patient he had been speaking to pondered the doctor's

last impassioned words. As a result over time he too became a Christian. He survived the prison camp and went on to tell the world what he had learned there.

The patient's name was Alexander Solzhenitsyn.

'As it is written: "How beautiful are the feet of those who bring good news.'

7

When God is Embraced

The need for effective grace, Acts 16:11–15

Jack was concerned about his non-Christian friend Joe. He so wanted him to become a believer. That is why every night before he turned in he knelt by his bedside to pray. His prayers for Joe always took the same form: 'Dear Lord, it would be wonderful if Joe became a Christian. I pray that somehow his IQ might be increased so that he will have the intelligence to see how reasonable and compelling the Christian faith is. Lord, if only you could work it so that Joe would come across a really good Gospel communicator. It would be terrific if you could see your way to getting Billy Graham to give him a call! Lord, if only Joe could be helped to make more of an *effort* to believe. But I know that at the end of the day, it is all down to him, so please don't do anything which will *make* him become a Christian and so compromise his free will.'

Is that how Christians pray? Of course not, although to hear some Christians speak you would think they should. Isn't the way we pray for those we long to see come to a saving faith in Christ something more along these lines: 'Heavenly Father, please open the eyes and soften the heart of Joe so that he may come to know you through your Son. As the Christian message is explained to him, give him the grace to repent and believe.'

As we have been seeing throughout our study of the great Biblical doctrines about the nature of God and man; human beings are by nature a pretty rebellious lot, 'Barbarousness always lurks at some level beneath [human nature]' writes the social critic, Os Guinness, 'Call the problem "original sin." as theologians have from the record of the Bible; call it the "crooked timber" of our humanity, as Immanuel Kant and Isaiah Berlin did; call it "dissonance in human form" as Nietzsche did; or call it "man's smudge" on the world, as poet Gerard Manley Hopkins did.'[1] Idolatry and Promethean pride often blind us to our need and set us against God's provision. While the call to Gospel proclamation is clear and compelling as we saw in the last chapter, on a purely human reckoning the task of persuading someone of the truth of the Christian faith to be accompanied by a willingness to submit to the rule of Christ would seem nigh on impossible.

But anyone who is at all familiar with the Bible and aware of their own nature knows only too well that the ultimate

---

1. Os Guinness, *Renaissance: the Power of the Gospel However Dark the Times* (IVP, Illinois, 2014), p. 16.

evangelist is God himself—God the Holy Spirit. He alone has the power to grant faith, to bring into being Christian believers, enabling them to be 'born again'. If Christians are not going to become frustrated as they share the Christian faith, or become tempted to employ some form psychological manipulation or coercion, then it is vital to hold on to this truth that *God* is the evangelist.[2]

It might be worth heading off a basic misunderstanding that some people raise at this point, namely, that if conversion is the work of God, then why employ any arguments at all?

Probably one of the greatest evangelists the world has ever known in post-apostolic times is the 18th century preacher, George Whitefield. Under his ministry thousands came to a genuine and living faith on both sides of the Atlantic. He was someone who held to the Bible's portrayal of a person's helplessness before God and God's sovereignty in reaching out to them. In his magisterial sermon, *'The Potter and the Clay'*, he says,

> If it be inquired who is to be the potter? And by whose agency this marred clay is to be formed into another vessel? Or in other words, if it be asked, how this great and mighty change is to be effected? I answer, not by mere dint and force of moral persuasion. This is good in its place. And I am so far from thinking, that Christian preachers should not make

---

2. Which is the title of a book which provides an excellent treatment of this subject, David F Wells, *God the Evangelist: How the Holy Spirit works to Bring Men and Women to Faith* (Authentic Media, 2000).

use of rational arguments and motives in their sermons, that
I cannot think they are fit to preach at all, who either cannot,
or will not use them. All this we readily grant. But at the same
time, I would as soon go to yonder church-yard and attempt
to raise the dead carcasses, with a 'come forth', as to preach to
dead souls, did I not hope for some superior power to make
the word effectual to the designed end. I should only be like
a sounding brass for any saving purposes, or as a tinkling
cymbal. Neither is this change to be wrought by the power
of our own free-will. This is an idol everywhere set up but we
dare not fall down and worship it. 'No man (says Christ) can
come to me, unless the Father draw him.' Our own free-will,
if improved, may restrain us from the commission of many
evils and put us in the way of conversion. But after exerting
our utmost efforts (and we are bound in duty to exert them)
we shall find the words of our own church articles to be true,
that 'man since the Fall hath no power to turn to God' ... I
inform you, that this heavenly potter, this blessed agent, is the
Almighty Spirit of God, the Holy Ghost, the third person in
the most adorable Trinity, co-essential with the Father and the
Son.[3]

We shall take up the issue of 'free will' a little later on, but at
this point it needs to be made clear that we don't have to opt
for an 'either-or' in our understanding of Gospel sharing—
either, all of God (and so we need do nothing) or all of man

---

3. George Whitefield, 'The Potter and the Clay', in *The Sermons of George Whitefield* 2 Vols. (ed. Lee Gatiss, The Reformed Evangelical Anglican Library, 2010), Vol. 1, pp. 258–259.

(and God remains weightless waiting on the sidelines for human beings to take the initiative).

One of the most delightful episodes in the New Testament which illustrates God's grace in eliciting saving faith is to be found in Act 16. It concerns an entrepreneur in the textile industry by the name of Lydia.

A divine action

In Luke's account, Paul and his companions arrive in the Roman colony of Philippi. His usual practice is to head for the local synagogue in order to present Jesus as the longed for Messiah. It would seem that in this instance no such synagogue exists. And so Paul heads out to a place he would expect to find a group of Jews in prayer on the Sabbath—by the river. Lo and behold, there is such a gathering and Paul presents the Gospel message. In verse 14 we then read, 'One of those listening was a woman named Lydia, a dealer in purple cloth from the city of Thyatira, who was a worshipper God. The *Lord* opened her heart to respond to Paul's message.'

Evangelistic speakers sometimes talk as if the door handle to our hearts was on the inside. Accordingly, they speak about *us* opening our hearts to Jesus. In one sense that is quite right, that certainly is what it *feels* like, a voluntary self-surrender to the Lord Jesus Christ. But that is not what Luke, under the inspiration of the Holy Spirit, writes here. He does not say, '*Lydia* opened her heart to Paul's message.' But 'the *Lord* opened her heart.' Who is the Lord? Given that later in v. 15 she speaks of herself as having become a believer in the

Lord, and since Paul has been speaking about Jesus, it follows that the one who has opened her heart to respond to Paul's message is none other than Jesus himself, whom as we saw in chapter 5 now operates on earth through the agency of his Holy Spirit.

What is going on is something like this: as Paul explains who Jesus is and what he came to do, the Lord by His Spirit *at the same time* is working to make the penny drop. God is not savingly at work *independently* of his Gospel message, but working *through* the Gospel message, bringing understanding and faith together and so enabling Lydia to believe.

It is at this point we might ask, 'What about free will? Isn't Lydia, or anyone else for that matter, free to believe or not believe, to choose or not choose to become a Christian?' The answer given to that question will all depend upon what we mean by the term 'free will'.

We are free to be what we are by nature and *not* free to be other than what we are. By nature dogs growl, the dog can't complain that he is not free to meow like a cat, because he isn't a cat, he's a dog. So the question we need to ask is: according to the Bible what are human beings like, spiritually, according to *their* nature? The answer is to be found in verses like these: Romans 8:7 'The natural, fleshly mind *is* enmity to God. It does not submit to God's law, *nor can it do so.*' 1 Corinthians 2:14 'The man without the Spirit does not accept the things that come from the Spirit of God, for they are foolishness to him, and *he cannot* understand them.' 2 Corinthians 4:3 'Even if our gospel is veiled, it is veiled to those who are perishing. The god of this age has *blinded* the *minds* of unbelievers.' And just in case you think these are the morbid musings of the apostle Paul, here is Jesus on the subject, John 6:44: 'No one can come to me *unless* the Father draws him.'

We *are* free to act in line with our nature and that nature is one which says, 'No' to God. I don't *want* you in my life, I want to run it independently of you.' We may not always put it as crudely as that but that is what it amounts to. Our hearts lock God out. We willingly affirm these rebellious hearts of ours. The problem, then, is not a matter of the intellect, or communication or will, as Jack in our parable thinks and so prays, the real problem is a hard, rebellious heart.

Let's get a little philosophical for a moment.

What has just been outlined is what is called the 'voluntarist' view of freedom (sometimes called 'freedom of inclination'). This was espoused by a friend of George Whitefield, the American theologian, Jonathan Edwards who argued that we simply choose according to our nature, that is we do what we *want* to do. More recently, Sam Storms has summarised this understanding as: 'The ability to act according to inclinations and desires without being compelled to do otherwise by something or someone external to himself.'[4]

---

4. Sam Storms, *Chosen for Life* (Crossway, 2007), pp. 59–63. This is to be distinguished from another view of freedom called 'libertarianism': 'An agent is free with respect to a given action at a given time if at that time it is within the

Living in our post-enlightenment and post-modern West, we may not particularly like this teaching but I would suggest that no other explanation will do to account for why the masses are still outside the churches. Just think about it. I know that some churches are dull and give you the creeps, but that aside, if men and women were just *neutral* regarding the Christian faith, on a pure statistical basis would we not expect to see more than a few point percent of the population attending church on a Sunday? People are not that reluctant about 'shop till they drop', or going to the pub or the cinema. If men and women had even the slightest warmth towards the God, should we not see our churches packed with people wanting to find out more about him? And even then we would only be accommodating a small proportion of the population. But we don't see that. Have you ever wondered why? Here is the explanation. We are not neutral. We are not mildly disposed towards God. Our hearts by their *nature* exclude him; the door has been slammed tight and the key thrown away. We simply do not *want* God in our lives on his own terms. That's our nature and so we act in line with it What is more, we do so willingly and are therefore responsible.

Here, then, is the big problem:

If spiritually *we cannot* and *do not* want to open our hearts

---

agent's power to perform the action and also the agent's power to refrain from the action' (William Hasker, 'A Philosophical Perspective', in Pinnock et al, *The Openness of God: A Biblical Challenge to the Traditional Understanding of God* [InterVarsity Press, 1994] pp. 136–137. We would contend that this view does not do justice either to the Biblical revelation or human experience.

to the Gospel then who is able to do it? It certainly will not be a weightless God! But the God who has revealed himself as supreme and triune can and does work this miracle. On the basis of what we have seen so far of the character of God, we will not be surprised to discover that there is nothing forceful about the way God opens our hearts. This is the way C. H Spurgeon describes this 'opening': 'When you see a casket wrenched open, the hinges torn off, the clasp destroyed, then you discern at once the hand of the thief. But when you observe the casket deftly and smoothly opened, with a master key, you discern the hand of the owner.' In the same way, he says, conversion isn't a violent wrenching open of the human heart in which the will and the reason are ignored or crushed. God opens hearts not like a beast with his prey, but like an owner with his treasure. He is not some cosmic rapist who forces himself upon us; he is the lover who gently woos us. He does not enslave the will, he frees it.

The night that I became convinced that I should become a Christian, with the result that I knelt down and surrendered my life to Christ, was the freest decision I had ever made. But I have no doubt that it was *God* who kindly enabled me to do it and therefore he receives all the glory. This is what is sometimes called *irresistible* or *effectual* grace—the Holy Spirit making effective in our hearts Christ's work on the cross. That is when we say from the heart that he died for *me*; it becomes close up and personal.

What is decisive is not our free will but God's free grace.

What this entails can be illustrated by the story told by Dr J. I. Packer of something which happened to him.

He related how, when he was a student at Oxford University, he had gone punting on the river and had fallen head first into the River Thames. He said it was a dreadful experience; the water was cold, murky and deep. What is more, his arms and legs had become entangled in a mass of thick weeds. For a while he thought he was finished. He then imagined what his fellow students who were still in the punt might have said.

One could have called out: 'You will be all right. You can get out of the water if you want to. Just keep on struggling and eventually you will make it.' A second might have said: 'I would like to help you, but I do have a problem with my conscience for I don't want to interfere with your free will. But I can give you some tips about swimming if you like.'

Those two imagined reactions parallel two views of how we obtain salvation in Christ which have appeared in different guises throughout the history of the church. One is called Pelagianism, the other Arminianism. Both believe that the work of Jesus upon the cross is vitally important and central for our salvation. But both believe that for that work to become effective in our lives we have to make a contribution of our own. Christ's death is necessary but not wholly sufficient to ensure our personal salvation. What is also necessary is our own self-generated faith; whereas the apostle Paul insists that this itself is a gift of God as it is not natural to us (Ephesians 2:8).

The Pelagian believes that we all have a natural ability to believe if we want to; our fallen nature, what the Bible calls 'the flesh' (*sarx*), is not a barrier. Indeed, it is within our nature to believe as a matter of the will.

Arminianism is a little different in that it readily agrees that supernatural help is required for us to believe the gospel (the 'work of the Holy Spirit speaking through his Word'), but this is open to everyone and can be resisted if we so choose.

In both cases God is dependent upon us choosing to respond to him. In one way or another both amount to saying: 'If you want to be saved you have to make the final step, God can only go so far, you have to do the rest.' But what if our spiritual state is akin to the physical state Dr Packer found himself in, drowning, and self-effort isn't enough?

Dr Packer developed the illustration further. When he fell into the river, he was immensely glad that the people in the punt were neither Pelagian nor Arminian, but Calvinists (those who uphold the sovereign providence of God covering all things). What actually happened was that a friend of his jumped into the river, overcame his hapless struggles, pulled him free of the reeds, brought him back to the shore, gave him artificial resuscitation and revived him. 'That,' said Dr Packer, 'is what I call a rescue!'[5]

---

5. Cited in Melvin Tinker, *Intended for Good: The Providence of God* (Inter Varsity Press, 2012), p. 143.

Given what the Bible teaches about the hostility of human nature to God, which is confirmed by experience, if I did not believe that God can and does open human hearts, I would leave the ministry tomorrow. I simply could not carry on because it would be an impossible task. But I do believe it and that is why I can pray with confidence for non-Christian friends and family that God would perform this miracle of open heart surgery. Not praying that they might believe in 'God', Lydia already had that belief before she met Paul according to v. 14, but rather that they might come to have a *saving* faith in God through Jesus Christ.

It is important that we understand that 'religion' never saved anybody—not even Lydia who is described as a 'worshipper', only Jesus can do that and nothing short of a supernatural operation in people's hearts is able to bring it about. This is why it is such great event when someone becomes a Christian and why it is a cause for celebration. Jesus says that there is 'rejoicing in the presence of the angels of God over one sinner who repents' (Luke 15:10). Just think about that for a moment. Whose presence are the angels in? It is *God's* presence, which means that it is *God* who is beside himself with joy when someone comes to know his Son as Saviour. If God is excited about it, then surely we should be excited about it too.

There are two extremes we must avoid.

There is what is called the hyper-Calvinist and the hyper-Charismatic.

The hyper-Calvinist says: 'If God is going to convert anybody, he will do it without our aid —after all *he* opens hearts not us.' So forget evangelism. On the other hand the hyper-charismatic says, 'It is the Holy Spirit who converts people, just so long as we pray for the Holy Spirit to work, who needs to *explain* the Gospel?' Thus we have the late Christian leader John Wimber, founder of the Vineyard movement, who relates how a non-Christian had what he called a 'power encounter', that is, he fell down on the floor after someone had laid hands on him. But when he got up, says Wimber he was a believer without anyone having explained to him what the Gospel was.[6] That simply can't be. As we shall see, God uses people like us to bring the Gospel *message* to people.

A determined strategy

Belief in God's sovereignty does not mean that we should not be thinking. What is striking in this account is how well thought-out Paul is in his approach.

In v. 13 we read that Luke, Paul, and a few others went outside the city to a river bank where they expected to find a place of prayer and accordingly found a group of women praying. As we have seen, Paul's normal strategy was to head for the Jewish synagogue and begin with the people there. In Philippi there wasn't one; maybe because there were not enough Jewish men in the city because you needed a quorum of ten Jewish men to start one. As a result, some

---

6. John Wimber and Kevin Springer, *Power Evangelism: Signs and Wonders Today* (Hodder and Stoughton, 1985).

adherents to the Jewish faith, mainly women, did the next best thing and held a prayer meeting, which is what is going on here which Paul and his friends happily gate crash. But there is 'method in his madness'. It makes sense to talk with folk who have at least *some* prior understanding of the faith, remembering here that the Christian faith arose out of and fulfilled the *Jewish* faith. In other words, it makes sense to begin with warm contacts, people we would perhaps refer to as 'nominal Christians', folk who show *some* interest, having some connection with the church.

This may be regarded as pragmatic, but it is plain common sense. As we begin with fringe members, folk who are mildly open to the Christian faith and, as by God's grace they are converted, then then the number of Gospel workers is steadily built up to reach out into the wider circle of the unchurched. Of course that doesn't mean we *exclusively* focus on them, not at all—we will want anybody and everybody to hear about Christ. But strategically it is sound.

We should notice too that Paul worked with what he had— he happily submitted to God's providential hand. He didn't take one look at the gathering and say to his colleagues, 'Well, fellers, not much going here, only a few women, let's move on and try and hit the big time by going to the next town.' No. God is sovereign and so providentially led Paul and his band to this place. What is more, God is concerned with *individuals;* he loves them and wants them to hear his saving message. As a Christian speaker I have to say it is all too easy to be dazzled by the crowd—so you can find time to speak at the big meeting, but not to old Mr Jones sitting by the fireside. That should not be. As well as being strategic we need to be opportunistic.

We are not to miss the obvious fact that Paul did actually relay a *message*—v. 13, 'We sat down and began *to speak*'. Then, v. 14, 'Lydia responded to Paul's *message.*' That is what evangelism *is*—explaining the message of Gospel. If that happens people are evangelised, if it doesn't, they aren't, no matter how moved and impressed they may be by the sincerity of our lives.

Sometimes you will see a wayside pulpit displaying the alleged words of Francis of Assisi, 'Preach the Gospel at all times, and when necessary, use words.' But as Os Guinness pointed out, that makes as much sense as saying, 'Feed people and when necessary use food.' Preaching the Gospel *means* using words. To be sure it is to be backed up by our lives too, but it is nothing less than that.

In his classic book, *Evangelism and the Sovereignty of God,* Dr J. I. Packer, writes,

How, then, should evangelism be defined? The New Testament answer is very simple. According to the New Testament, evangelism is just preaching the gospel, the evangel. It is a work of communication in which Christians make themselves mouthpieces for God's message of mercy to sinners. Anyone who faithfully delivers that message, under whatever circumstances, in a large meeting, in a small meeting, from a pulpit, or in a private conversation, is evangelizing.[7]

That is exactly what we see Paul doing at Philippi and it behooves us to do the same.

A dedicated response

Are there any visible indications to an authentic response to the Gospel message? Indeed there are as we see in v. 15, 'When she and the members of her household were baptised, she invited us to her home. "If you consider me a believer in the Lord," she said, "come and stay at my house." And she persuaded us.'

An open heart invariably leads to an open home. How do we know that the Lord has opened our hearts? Is it because we can recite certain truths? Or maybe sing certain songs? Perhaps we can look back to some special event when we committed our life to Christ? It could be some or all of these things. But one clear indicator the Bible gives of genuine, authentic conversion is what the apostle John calls 'Love of the brethren.' (1 John 4:7ff). It is that down-to-earth love of fellow Christians. This is what we see happening here with Lydia.

We need to understand that in this kind of culture, table

---

7. J. I. Packer, *Evangelism and the Sovereignty of* God (Downers Grove, IL: IVP, 1991), p. 41.

fellowship (hospitality) was a sign of full social acceptance.[8] There is a sense in which Christians should be in and out of each other's homes. Not as busy bodies, but showing hospitality as a sign of true Christian love. At the very least if you are a true believer you will want to be with your fellow believers in church on a Sunday in wanting to pray together, praise together and talk about the things of God together.

Luke says that Lydia, '*persuaded* us'. Lydia, who might have been quite a formidable lady, wouldn't take 'no' for an answer—and neither should we.

Genuine faith leads to genuine fellowship with the genuine God and his people.

---

8. See Kenneth Bailey, *Jesus Through Middle-Eastern Eyes* (Downers Grove, IL: IVP, 2008), Chapter 18.

8

When God Returns

The Necessity of the Second Coming, 2 Peter 3

For many people today their view about the future could be summed up by the song from the musical, 'Paint Your Wagon': 'Where am I going, I don't know, where am I heading, I ain't certain, all that I know is I am on my way.'

What we think is going to be our future will affect how we live in the present. This in turn is shaped by what we understand the universe ultimately to be at 'rock bottom'. For the greater part of the late Twentieth century, the philosophy of materialism tended to dominate. This view is summed up by Dallas Willard as, 'There is one reality, the natural world, and physics is its prophet.'[1] If life, the universe and

---

1. Dallas Willard, "What Significance Has Postmodernism for The Christian Faith?," http://www.dwillard.org/articles/artview.asp?artID=70

everything, is nothing more than the product of blind, impersonal, meaningless forces, such that we come from nowhere and are heading nowhere—then where does that leave us? The answer is ... nowhere in the purpose-of-life stakes.

The comedian Woody Allen, in one of his more reflective moods, put the human predicament without God quite accurately when he said, 'Alienation, loneliness and emptiness verging on madness .... the fundamental thing behind all motivation and all activity is the constant struggle against annihilation and death. It is absolutely stupefying in its terror and it renders anyone's accomplishments meaningless. It's not only that he the individual dies, or that man as a whole dies, but that you struggle to do a work of art that will last and then you realise that the universe itself is not going to exist after a period of time.' And then he adds, 'Until those issues are resolved in each person—religiously, psychologically or existentially—the social and political issues will never be resolved, except in a slapdash way.'[2] Allen is quite correct. Either life is 'a tale told by an idiot, full of sound and fury' and therefore 'hope' is a word devoid of meaning *or* what the Bible teaches is true, namely, that the universe is the work of a glorious, loving Creator, whose signature is written in the heavens he has made and the knowledge of whose existence reverberates deep down in our hearts. This Divine Author has declared that we do matter and that the whole

---

2. Cited in Francis Schaeffer and Koop C. Everett, *Whatever Happened to the Human Race?* (London: Marshall, Morgan and Scott, 1980), pp. 97–98.

history is moving towards one dramatic climactic event—the return of Jesus Christ.

A passage in the Bible which spells this out for us with breathtaking clarity is 2 Peter, chapter 3.

Back to the Future

In the spectrum of world faiths Christianity has a unique appreciation of the future. It is not like so much of Greek Philosophy which views history as cyclical, just repeating itself endlessly—Pythagoras, for example, believed in reincarnation. Or like Hinduism which declares that what we consider to be reality is in fact 'maya'—illusion. Here we all get caught up on the wheel of 'samsara' with our lives being repeated by reincarnation until we all dissolve in the sea of nothingness called Nirvana. Christianity teaches something quite different, namely, that the passage of time is purposeful and God-directed—we are actually heading somewhere. We are all on a journey with a specific destination in view. The Christian message isn't just about having 'Jesus in your heart' while you live, nor is it simply a message about 'going to heaven' when you die. According to v. 13 it involves a new heaven and a new earth which in one universal shattering future event will replace this old, corrupt, weary world of ours: 'But in keeping with his promise we are looking forward to a new heaven and a new earth, where righteousness dwells.'

N.T. Wright draws attention to how this doctrine gives shape and balance to the Christian worldview thus making it so distinctive:

Like the Jewish worldview, but radically different to the Stoic, the Platonic, the Hindu, and the Buddhist worldviews, the Christian worldview is a story with a beginning, a middle and an end. Not to have closure at the end of the story—to be left with a potentially endless cycle, round and round with either the same things happening again and again or simply perhaps the long outworking of karma would be the very antithesis of the story told by the apostles and by the long line of their Jewish predecessors.[3]

The Moody Blues

It is interesting to note how moods and trends change amongst groups of people during the course of history. Throughout the 19th and well into the 20th centuries optimism was in the ascendant in the West. This is to be distinguished from what is the main focus of this passage of Peter which is *hope*:

The reality is one of hope, not optimism. For the last two or three centuries the Western world had been nurtured on a belief in Progress. Despite all the evidence to the contrary, we have been taught to believe that the world is getting better and better. Industrial progress, technological innovation, and the many-sided wisdom of the Enlightenment, have produced and will produce a world in which the old evils will be left behind.[4]

---

3. N. T. Wright, *Surprised by Hope: Rethinking Heaven, the Resurrection and the Mission of the Church* (Harper Collins, 2007), p. 107.

4. N. T. Wright, *The Millennium Myth: Hope for the Postmodern World* (Westminster John Knox Press, 199), p. 39.

It would be fair to say that today the mood of optimism has been exchanged for pessimism coupled with cynicism with regards to the future. The breezy optimism of the 19th century which spilled over into much of the 20th century has given way to the 'uncertain-live-for-now-pessimism' of the 21st century. This has been compounded by the complex phenomenon known as 'postmodernism'. With the abandonment of the belief that the world can be understood to have an 'over-arching story' (metanarrative), it is simply nonsense to think of future hope, for that implies purpose and direction as in a story. Instead, we are left living in a fragmented, directionless world.

All we are left with, then, is a plurality of stories—your story, my story. You're Ok and I'm Ok (or not as the case may be), but the stories don't need to intersect or interact. Metanarratives are deemed to be oppressive; freedom consists in telling and living by our own mini-stories, our own local stories. This, inevitably, produces a world in which everyone tells their own individual story, often in increasing isolation. Nor is this the end of the process. The individual tells different stories about him or herself at different times, and even perhaps lives in various overlapping but incompatible stories simultaneously. The result is known, notoriously, as deconstruction.[5]

Pessimism and despair is at the end of the line.[6]

---

5. N. T. Wright, *The Millennium Myth: Hope for the Postmodern World*, p. 59.

6. Woody Allen's answer to this lack of meaning is to create our own, 'The universe is indifferent ... so we create a fake world for ourselves, and we exist

It may come as a bit of a surprise to discover that it was rather like this in Peter's day too, 'In the last days (that is, the period between Jesus' first appearance and his second appearance) scoffers will come and following their own evil desires will say 'Where is this coming?''' (v3).

'Things haven't changed much' the sceptics argue, 'the world is the 'same old same old'. We still have wars. We have natural disasters. Crime is still rampant. Why doesn't God do something if he is going to do anything at all? Perhaps he can't? Perhaps he won't. Maybe he just doesn't care? Perhaps he simply doesn't exist'. Today we find ourselves in a situation where even leaders within our churches have given up on the belief that there will be a second coming. Such outmoded ideas are seen to be the stuff of cranks and sandwich-board carriers, they say, not the belief of sophisticated people who have science and technology at their disposal.

But is such a belief that hard to accept? There is nothing unreasonable and everything wholly sensible to believe that the One who made and owns this world and who 2000 years ago entered into the slipstream of history as a human being—Jesus of Nazareth—should one day come back to wind up the whole show and give dignity to our existence by calling us to give an account to him.

within that fake world ... a world that, in fact, means nothing at all, when you step back. It's meaningless. But it's important that we create some sense of meaning, because no perceptible meaning exists for anybody." Interview with Stig Björkman, *Woody Allen on Woody Allen* (New York: Grove Press, 1993).

Can't believe or won't believe?

Peter is candid enough to tell us that the reason some find it difficult to believe is not primarily intellectual but moral— people just don't *want* to believe it. If we are honest many of us are simply not enamoured with the idea that we are made by someone and are therefore accountable to someone. The real problem, argues Peter, is that we are being led astray by our own evil *desires*. It is not that belief in the second coming is intellectually indefensible; rather it is that it is morally uncomfortable and we would rather live as if the judgement day is not going to happen. One is reminded of the saying of G. K. Chesterton that 'It is not that Christianity has been tried and found wanting, but rather that it has been found demanding and therefore not tried.'

Sometimes the impression is given by the militant atheist that his atheism is the result of long, sustained, rigorous, intellectual thought. But one might want to consider whether there are deeper, ulterior motives at work resulting in not *wanting* to believe. One atheist who was quite candid that this was so for himself, was the author of *Brave New World*, Aldous Huxley:

> For myself, as, no doubt for most of my contemporaries, the philosophy of meaninglessness was essentially an instrument of liberation. The liberation we desired was simultaneously liberation from a certain political and economic system and liberation from a certain system of morality. We objected to the morality because it interfered with our sexual freedom; we objected to the political and economic system because it was unjust. The supporters of these systems claimed that in

some way they embodied meaning (a Christian meaning, they insisted) of the world. There was one admirably simple method of confuting these people and at the same time justifying ourselves in our political and erotic revolt: We could deny that the world had any meaning whatsoever.[7]

Huxley elsewhere was even more open in his admission of ulterior motives, 'Those who detect no meaning in the world generally do so because, for one reason or another, it suits their books that the world should be meaningless.'[8]

Back to the Bible

The most fundamental thing such sceptics turn a blind eye to, argues Peter, is the *unanimous testimony of the Bible*.

Peter tells us that he is not saying anything new, verses 1–2, 'Dear friends, this is now my second letter to you. I have written both of them as reminders to stimulate you to wholesome thinking. I want you to *recall* the words spoken in the past by the holy prophets and the command given by our Lord and Saviour through your apostles.'

From Genesis to Revelation the Bible makes it quite plain that God through his appointed ruler-—'the Christ'—is going to set up his eternal reign of righteous love. That is the thrust of verses 1–2. Wherever you look in the Bible, whether it is the prophets in the Old Testament, the apostles in the New or the teaching of Jesus himself; the testimony is consistent—

---

7. Aldous Huxley, *Ends and Means* (Chatto & Windus, 1946), p. 273.
8. *Ends and Means*, p. 270.

Christ is coming and therefore we had better be prepared to meet him.

I was quite taken by an interview John Humphreys of BBC Radio 4's 'Today' programme undertook a few years ago with the Ulster politician and preacher, Dr Ian Paisley which was repeated the day after he died. John Humphreys said something along the lines, 'When I meet God or *if* I meet him ...' Immediately Paisley interjected, 'Of that there is no doubt, you *will* meet him as we all shall meet him and have to give an account for the way we have lived.' It is the only time I have heard John Humphreys flummoxed in an interview! In the rest of the passage Peter backs up this claim that we are all going to meet Christ one day. In v. 5 he refers to Genesis 1 and creation; in v. 6—Genesis 6 and the flood; v. 7, innumerable OT prophecies; v. 8, he quotes Psalm 90, and in v. 10, he refers to Luke's Gospel and a saying of Jesus that his return will be like a thief in the night. In v. 13 he implicitly refers to Isaiah 65 which talks of a new heaven and earth. We can't pick and choose with the Bible, taking out one bit about God loving us and saying I will have that and leaving out the more unpalatable bits about God judging us. It is a seamless garment, take out one major doctrine and the rest unravels.

There are three special relationships that God has which the Bible tells us about concerning the theme of the end of the world.

God and History

First, it tells us something about the relationship between God and history. In v. 5-6, Peter refers to Noah's flood.

The point being made is this: God acts *in* history—and he
does so in salvation and judgement. He is not a God who
wound up the world, setting it in motion and then retired
like some disinterested cosmic clock maker. The one true
God is *personally* involved in the world he has made. In fact
he not only meets us daily with blessing; 'causing the sun to
shine on the just and unjust alike' (Matthew 5:45), but also
in retributive judgement (Romans 1:18ff). If we are foolish
enough to thumb our noses at our Creator and treat each
other and his world with disdain, do we honestly think for a
moment that he will idly sit back and let it happen without
any consequences? He will not. God will hand us over to
the inevitable effects of our practical atheism as two World
Wars tragically show and as the moral and social demise of
our own society demonstrate only all too clearly. Say 'good-
bye' to God and you can say 'good-bye' to social stability.
It happens every time. History is just that, '*His*-story.' It's
as much about God rolling up his sleeves and getting stuck
into the affairs of human beings as it is us doing all we can
to thwart his purposes. If God is working in history then it
makes perfect sense that he will guide it to a grand conclusion
with one great, climactic scene before the final curtain comes
down.

What is more, this is achieved by divine command. It is all
about God's Word, 'But they (the sceptics) deliberately forget
that long ago by God's *word* the heavens existed and the earth
was formed out of water and by water. By these waters also
the world of that time was deluged and destroyed. By the
same *word* the present heavens and earth are reserved for

fire, being kept for the day of judgment and destruction of ungodly men.' (2 Peter 3:5–7)

God creates by his Word, he judges by his Word, he saves by his Word (the word of the Gospel) and God will *keep* his Word—he will return to save and judge.

God and Time
Secondly, Peter tells us about the Bible's view of God and time—v. 8, 'With the Lord a day is like a thousand years, and a thousand years are like a day.'

Let us think about this.

Time can only be measured in an arena where change takes place. Our bodies grow old; our cars wear out, rivers flow to the sea. But supposing we lived in a world which was changeless. Suppose our eyes could not only move left and right, but backwards and forwards in *time,* so we could perceive the horizons of history as well as the horizons of our globe? In short, what if we lived in eternity? What would our time look like from that perspective? Then such a being would see everything within 'one eternal moment' and would plan with 'everything in view', as he sees the 'end from the beginning'. Nothing would take him by surprise and so nothing would be left to 'chance'. Like the mind of an author conceiving a book, all the characters and their histories appear in his mind at once, their past, present and future are seen together in the eternal 'Now'. Why should this not be the case with God and the world?[9]

To enable us to grasp how we might begin to conceive this relationship between a timeless God and creatures like ourselves who are bound by time, C. S Lewis suggests the following:

> If you picture Time as a straight line along which we have to travel, then you must picture God as the whole page on which the line is drawn. We come to the parts of the line one by one: we have to leave A behind before we get to B, and we cannot reach C until we leave B behind. God, from above or outside or all round, contains the whole line, and sees all.[10]

This means that God is not thwarted by anything we might

---

9. This view of the timelessness of God has a rich Christian heritage. Here is Boethius, 'It is the common judgement, then, of all creatures that live by reason that God is eternal. So let us consider the nature of eternity, for this will make clear to us both the nature of God and his manner of knowing. Eternity, then, is the complete, simultaneous and perfect possession of everlasting life ... And if human and divine present may be compared, just as you see certain things in this your present time, so God sees all things in His eternal present.' Boethius, *Consolation of Philosophy*, Book 5, Translated E. V. Watts (Harmondsworth: Penguin Classics, 1969). It is quite clear that Boethius was a major influence on the thinking of C. S. Lewis in this area, e.g. *Mere Christianity* (Book 4, Chapter 3). Aquinas says something similar, 'God's knowledge, like his existence, is measured by eternity, which in one and the same instant encompasses all time; so his gaze is eternally focused on everything in time as on something present ... What happens in time is known by us in time, moment by moment, but by God in an eternal moment, above time.' Thomas Aquinas, *Summa Theologica*, Timothy McDermott (ed.) A Concise Translation (London: Methuen, 1991).

10. C. S. Lewis, *Mere Christianity* (Fount, 1978), p.144.

do, and so having to say, 'Oh dear, I didn't quite see that one coming! What am I going to do next?' He is God, the eternal one. So whether it is five seconds or five millennia, from the standpoint of his plans it's all the same to him. This truth is meant to reassure us—God is in control.

Does 2,000 years seem a long time? It is but a mere blink in the eye of eternity. Therefore we are not to be fooled into falsely thinking that because Jesus has not yet returned he never will return. As Peter remarks in v. 10, the day will come like a 'thief in the night'. The thief has made his plans, he knows which house he is going to burgle and at what time, and it would not be on for him to send a calling card beforehand! God is not going to send a calling card either, he expects us to be ready to meet him at anytime.

God's relationship with humanity

This brings us to the third and perhaps most important divine relationship—God's relationship with us—v. 9, 'The Lord is not slow in keeping his promise, as some understand slowness. He is *patient* with you, not wanting anyone to perish, but everyone to come to repentance.' As David Wells observes,

> God, in his patience, has not been quick to judge, though he could have so acted with full justification. But he waited. He waited until the plan of redemption had unfolded in the person and work of Christ his promises of mercy could be proclaimed

and accepted. He waited and then commanded repentance and belief in Christ. And still he waits.[11]

Back in 1970 I am sure that there were many Christians praying that Jesus would return. Personally, I am glad that God didn't answer their prayers. This is because in 1970 I wasn't a Christian. I wasn't ready to meet with my Maker, for morally and spiritually I was in deep trouble. Why hasn't Christ come back? For the simple reason that God is merciful and continues to hold out his gracious hand to rescue;

> Why does he [God] not obliterate the space in which sin and rebelliousness fester? Why does he not move quickly to terminate evil? Is it that he is unaware of what is happening in life? Does he not know what is happening in the church? Does he not know that there are places in the world today where persecution rages? Is he unaware that there are countries in which atheism had been made the official 'religion'? … How many people, in every age, have asked themselves these questions? I have myself, many times. So, what is the answer? 'You,' the psalmist declared, 'are a God merciful and gracious, slow to anger and abounding in steadfast love and faithfulness' (Ps. 86:15; Ps. 103:8).[12]

However we are not to make the mistake of thinking, 'I will leave making up my mind about the Christian faith until

---

11. David F Wells, *God in the Whirlwind: How the Holy-Love of God Reorients Our World* (Crossway, 2014), p. 96.

12. David F Wells, *God in the Whirlwind: How the Holy-Love of God Reorients Our World* (Crossway, 2014), p. 97.

some later date. I will live life to the full doing what *I* want and when I get *really* old, then I might give religion a go.' It doesn't work like that. If you set you heart against God now there is no guarantee your heart will be able to be opened up to him later, quite the reverse in fact, it gets *harder* not easier with the passage of time. Judgement deferred is not judgement denied.

What, then, is the point of this teaching about the Second coming? Is it to provide material for speculative books which sell in their millions as is happening with the Tim LaHaye *Left Behind* series, now made into a Hollywood movie starring Nick Cage? Or maybe it is a call for us to batten down the hatches and withdraw into our holy huddles because the world is going to get worse and worse and there is nothing we can do about it except wait for the Big End? Some Christians seem to think so. But the reason Peter gives is much more down-to-earth and practical, as we see in v. 11, 'Since everything will be destroyed in this way, *what kind of people ought you to be*? You ought to live holy and godly lives', and v. 14, 'So then, dear friends, since you are looking forward to this, make every effort to be found spotless, blameless and at peace with him' and again in v. 17. 'Therefore, dear friends, since you already know this, be on your guard so that you may not be carried away by the error of lawless men and fall from your secure position. But grow in the grace and knowledge of our Lord and Saviour Jesus Christ.'

'I do not think in the last 40 years I have lived one conscious hour that has not been influenced by our Lord's return.' So wrote Anthony Ashley Cooper, better known as Lord Shaftesbury. Shaftesbury probably did more to improve the welfare of the poor and disadvantaged than any other single person in the 19th century, hence him fondly being referred to as 'the poor man's Earl'. He tirelessly sought to reform the treatment of the insane, pioneered legislation against exploitation of labour in factories, sponsored low-cost urban housing and free education for destitute children. His view of the future affected his life in the present. He didn't want to waste his life, frittering it away with non-stop entertainment as many of us find ourselves doing today, for he knew one day he would appear before his Saviour and he wanted to hear those words which every Christian wants to hear, 'Well, done good and *faithful* servant.' He knew that what mattered, for he knew what was to be lasting and what was to be burned up. That new car, that new house, even that university degree, will not last; they belong to the old order and will be destroyed along with it.

What will go on into the new world? What will shield us from the shame of judgement? The answer is: character, holy lives designed to live in a holy world. If we are not concerned with personal holiness and using our gifts for God's glory now, then that just shows we are not serious about the world to come then. But if, like Shaftesbury, we are gripped with the thought and joy that one day Jesus is going to appear in dazzling glory, surrounded by angels, and we shall see him seated on his heavenly throne—we will want to be building our lives around that great reality, making every effort, as Peter says, to be found 'spotless, blameless and at peace' with him.

The film, *Flags of our Fathers* is a very moving, and at times harrowing, account of the Battle for Iwo Jima in the Pacific during World War 2. Many of the US Marines were teenagers, some seventeen, eighteen or nineteen years old. The island was defended by 22,000 Japanese soldiers, 21,000 of which were killed but at the cost of 26,000 US casualties. On one of the gravestones at the cemetery there, someone chiselled the message: 'When you go home, Tell them of us and say, For your tomorrow, We gave our today.' Can we think of a more fitting tribute for a Christian to be able to say, 'For your tomorrow, I gave my today'? Not just their tomorrows on earth but the countless tomorrows in eternity which get better and better with gladness in the love of Christ?

Just think of what some of those teenagers went through to secure our tomorrows. Here is an extract from one such account:

William Hoopes was crouching beside a medic named Kelly, who put his head above the protective ridge and places his binoculars to his eyes just for an instant ... in that instant a sniper shot him through the Adam's apple. Hoopes, a pharmacist's mate himself struggled frantically to save his friend ... Hoopes recalled 'His blood was spurting. He had not speech but his eyes were on me. He knew I was trying to save his life. I tried everything in the world. I couldn't do it. I tried. I couldn't get to the artery. I was trying so hard and all the while he just looked at me. The last thing he did as the blood spurts became less and less was to pat me on the arm as if to say, "That's all right." Then he died.'

John Piper commenting on this story says:

> In this heart-breaking moment I want to be Hoopes and
> I want to be Kelly. I want to be able to say to suffering and
> perishing people: 'I tried everything in the world ... I was
> trying so hard.' And I want to be able to say to those around me
> when I die, 'It's all right.'[13]

Looking forward to the 'tomorrow' of Christ's return and
a new heaven and earth, the Christian should unflinchingly
give of their 'today'.

---

13. John Piper, *Don't Waste Your Life* (Crossway, 2003), pp. 124–125.

9

When God makes all things new

The Need to be Heavenly Minded, Isaiah 65:17–25

In March 1997, 39 members of a group known as the 'Heaven's Gate', staged a bizarre mass suicide in an affluent community near San Diego, California. The cult members apparently believed that by taking their lives they would rendezvous with a spaceship hiding in the tail of comet Hale-Bopp, which was passing by Earth. The spaceship would then transport the faithful cult members to heaven.

At about the same time a poll was published which revealed that Canadians, who, according to the UN Human Development Index live in what the rest of the world finds to be the most desirable place on earth, are in fact 'in the grip of unprecedented national despair' and 'foresee a grim future' such that they have given up on traditional institutions such as government.

What these two news stories reveal in different ways is the fact that within Western society there is an increasing uncertainty about the future. Not all that long ago the prevailing belief was that through a combination of education, technology and moral enlightenment, Utopia was going to be achievable. There are still a few (and they are a few) who would cling on to that belief; and so for example Dr Desmond King-Hele concludes his book, *The End of the 20th Century* with these words:

> If war is avoided, if the hungry are fed, if the rise of the population is checked and the quality of living is improved by curbing pollution and building new towns to live in, we might advance to a marvellously fruitful era when the future wonders of science and technology will be exploited for the benefit of all.[1]

Did you notice how many 'if's were in there? But as we look at the news today such words tend to have a hollow ring to them.

It could be that what is called 'Generation X' –the post war baby-boomers—is the first generation in human history to be devoid of any belief which will enable them live in the present by having a clear view of the future. In his novel, 'Girlfriend in a Coma', Douglas Coupland, has one character expressing such anxiety in this way: 'There's darkness to the future ... the future's not a good place.'[2]

---

1. Desmond King-Hele, *The End of the 20th Century* (Macmillan, 1970).
2. Douglas Coupland, *Girlfriend in a Coma* (Harper Perennial, 2008).

There is, however, one group of people on this planet who above everything else *are* people of hope, namely, Christian believers. The reason for this is that woven into the fabric of the Bible's story line is that this world has an origin in God and also a future in God.

What we are given in Isaiah 65 is a glimpse of what that future entails. Invariably, figurative language is used, for how else can the prophet describe the indescribable but by drawing on aspects of our present life to create impressions of the future life? And that is what these are—impressions, for, as Paul Helm helpfully reminds us,

> The Bible does not set out to answer all our questions—the purpose of such teaching in Scripture is not to satisfy our curiosity, but to support our faith. The biblical writers do not try to fill in the gaps of our knowledge only to succeed in making a bad job of it. Rather the intention of the writers is to assure believers, not to inform them with encyclopaedic detail, that the life to come is certain and that it will be the climax of their deepest Christian hopes and longings.[3]

According to Isaiah in Chapter 65 that will be a future in which we shall be completely happy, v. 19; completely secure, v. 22; and completely at peace, v. 24. Under the inspiration of God's Spirit the prophet draws upon our own *present* experiences and contrasts them with what shall be our future experiences when this glorious transformation of the world

---

3. 'Paul Helm, *The Last Things* (Banner of Truth Trust, 1989), p. 87.

takes place, which, as we saw in the last chapter shall occur with the return of Jesus Christ.

Free at last

The first thing about this new world order is that it is a place where there is *freedom from sin*. We are told in v. 19 that God will *rejoice* over his New Jerusalem and take *delight* in his people. God would not be able to do that if it contained any blemish which spoiled or marred that which he has made. Back in Genesis 1:31 we read that when God created the heavens and the earth he pronounced it 'very good'. But this new creation is going to draw from God more than affirmation; it is going to draw forth celebration. This new city will be a delight and its people a joy, says Isaiah.

What a contrast with what the prophet describes at the beginning of his book. There we have an account of Jerusalem and its people which is anything but a delight: 'See how the faithful city has become a prostitute! She once was full of justice; righteousness used to dwell in her— but now murderers! Your silver has become dross, your choice wine is diluted with water. Your rulers are rebels, partners with thieves; they all love bribes and chase after gifts. They do not defend the cause of the fatherless; the widow's case does not come before them.' (Isaiah 1:23–26)

The city is a disgrace, it is a cesspit of moral corruption and decadence and its people are selfish and rebellious. Far from delighting God's heart the people break it. Instead of evoking commendation they receive condemnation.

In many ways that city represents our world on the run from its Maker. Therefore, we have to ask: what has happened between chapter 1 and chapter 65 to enable the prophet to look forward with such confidence to a new city and a new people being brought into being? The answer is to be found just over half way through the book where God promises to send his Servant whom we are told in chapter 53, will be led like a lamb to the slaughter, to hang on a scaffold, as God lays the iniquities of us all upon his delicate shoulders. He is the sacrificial guilt offering which bears away 'the sins of the world'. In other words, redemption is promised. What we see here in this chapter of Isaiah are some of the full fruits of that redemptive work: the formation of a renewed people purchased by the blood of his Servant to dwell *with* him into all eternity. However, what the prophet looked forward to in that central section, has now happened, for *Jesus* was that Servant. *He* is the Lord redeeming a people for himself and who is yet to come to consummate his everlasting kingdom.

As we glimpse the future portrayed by Isaiah we see a world in which the effects of sin are reversed and the old order of a world under the shadow of God's curse replaced by a new world dwelling in the light of God's blessing. This is because that which drew the curse, namely, sin, will be no more.

The death of death

In verse v. 20 we see one such reversal, 'Never again will there be in it an infant who lives but a few days or an old man who does not live out his years, he who dies at a hundred will be thought of as a mere youth.'[4]

One of the most poignant and painful reminders that we live in a world which has gone badly wrong is death. Nowhere is this more shattering than with the death of an infant. I have had to conduct such funerals and, quite frankly, it is devastating, for instinctively we cry out: 'This should not be!'

Some time ago my family and I visited Eyam in Derbyshire, the place where the Plague was stopped in 1666. One of the most moving pictures in the exhibition on display there is of a Mrs Hancock dragging the body of her dead husband along the ground by herself to be buried. What was even more disturbing was the information given beneath the picture that she had previously just buried her six children within the span of a few days.

At the time of Isaiah, infant mortality was much higher than in the modern day West. A single family could have four or five children who would not reach adulthood. To get beyond 45 years old was a major achievement. Yet for all our longevity death is the taboo subject of the 21st century, understandably so, for there is no answer to it. We might delay it, but we can't eradicate it. But that great terror will be no more in this new world. No infant will fail to enjoy life nor

---

4. It is possible that v. 20c should be translated, 'and the sinner, a hundred years old would be cursed' in which case note that judgement is still in view for the unrepentant, 'There is no escape for the sinner, even should he live to be a hundred the curse will catch him.' J. A. Motyer, *Isaiah by the Day* (Christian Focus, 2011), p. 310

an elderly person come short of total fulfilment. Indeed, you would be but a mere youth if you were to die at a hundred! This doesn't mean death will be present, it is simply a poetic way of saying that over the whole of life, young and old—the power of death will be destroyed.

This hope has served Christians well throughout the centuries since Christ's resurrection broke its tyrannical rule (1 Corinthians. 15:55–58).

Such was the case with the 16th century Reformer, Martin Luther.

He and his wife Katie had six children in all. They also took in four orphaned children. One child died near birth, another Magdalene, died at the age of 13. Magdalene was Luther's favourite daughter and her death almost drove him to despair, and would have done so had it not been for his Christian faith and the kind of vision offered here by Isaiah. As she lay dying, Luther weeping at her bedside asked her: 'Magdalene, my dear little daughter, would you like to stay here with your father or would you be willing to go to your Father yonder?' Magdalene answered: 'Darling father, as God wills.' Luther wept and holding her in his arms he prayed that God would free her and then she died. At the funeral service, (which Luther conducted), with his daughter laid out in the coffin, he declared: 'Darling Lena, you will rise and shine like a star, yea like the sun … I am happy in spirit but the flesh is sorrowful and weak and will not be content, the parting grieves me beyond measure. I have sent a saint to heaven.' No purgatory or 'ifs and buts' just the quiet certainty that God will keep his promise, 'whoever believes on him *shall* have eternal life'.

Secondly, the 'dis-ease' which characterises our world will be replaced with total harmony—so as it says in v. 25 what were natural enemies—wolves and lambs will lie down together. All that we can but dream of now will then become a reality.

Future Concerns

There are two worrying questions which Christians often raise which may, at least in part, be answered by this passage.

The first is: Will it be possible for us to sin again in the new heaven and new earth? If, when this world was originally made, perfect people sinned, could it not happen again in the new world?

The short answer is: No.

The reason is given in v. 24: 'Before they call I will answer; while they are still speaking I will hear.' This means that there is such complete oneness between God and his people that he anticipates their needs with a constant, providential watchfulness.[5] But more than that, it means there is such an identity between them, that while the people are *still* speaking, what they say immediately commends itself to God, i.e. what *they* want and what *he* wants are one and the

---

5. See J. A. Motyer, *The Prophecy of Isaiah* (Downers Grove, IL: InterVarsity Press, 1993), p. 531

same. This is because in the world to come we shall be given
new hearts and new minds devoid of any sin, such that we
shall never be out of sync with God. Or to put it another way:
We will not only not want to sin, but not want to want to sin
because we will be so reconstituted by God that we will be
incapable of it.

It is readily admitted that this idea is quite unacceptable
to the modern mind and, indeed even to some Christian
minds, who think of freedom as the ability to choose between
different courses of action—good and evil for example. But
that is not the biblical view of freedom. Freedom is the ability
to choose according to the truth, to do what we *ought* and not
just what we *want*. That was Jesus' position. He was tempted
and felt spiritual struggle just like us, but he *couldn't* sin, he
didn't want to.[6] If to have such a moral character that you
cannot sin and do not want to sin means you are not free,
then it follows that Jesus wasn't free, and neither is God the
Father for that matter, for he *cannot* sin. But it is a miserable
delusion and a pathetic idea of freedom to think that if only
God could succumb to temptation he would be free and not
otherwise![7] On the contrary, the glory of God, which makes
him the supreme object worthy of our worship and total
trust, is that he is *incapable* of change, unable and *unwilling*
to depart from the immaculate standards of his own majestic
holiness. And when we get to heaven, we will be like him in

---

6. Hebrews 4:15

7. This is the line of thought followed by the 'libertarian' view of freedom
discussed in chapter 7. However, adopting a voluntarist view would mean that
our new nature is such that our heavenly desires would be in line with that nature
meaning we would 'do what we want to do', namely, please God!

this respect—free to do only what is right ... and loving every minute of it![8]

The second worry Christians sometimes have is if, as we have seen in v. 19, heaven is a place of consummate joy, will not that joy be diminished to some degree by bad memories of what we have done while on earth or by thoughts of those who are not in heaven? A clue as to how this worry might be assuaged is contained in verse 17: 'The former things will *not* be remembered, *nor will they come to mind.*' 'Not be remembered' refers to the conscious contents of memory, 'come to mind', refers to memories suddenly aroused. This is suggestive that not only will *God* blot out the past, but so shall we. All the past troubles of this life, all the failures, and the pangs of consciences which disturb us now will not even come to our minds then, let alone to God's mind, in order to accuse us.[9]

Although we can't imagine it (and who can fully imagine any of this?), might we not reasonably speculate that such selective amnesia which applies to the old order of things will *include* those who, because of their refusal to embrace Christ's offer of salvation, are banished from his presence? Though such thoughts trouble us now, and so spur us on to pray for them and seek to share the gospel with them, following the logic of this passage through, they will *not*

---

8. For a development of this argument see, Paul Helm, *The Last Things* (Banner of Truth Trust, 1989), pp. 91–92.

9. 'The divine forgetfulness of v. 16 will be matched by general amnesia', J. A. Motyer, op. cit., p. 529.

trouble us in the new world because such thoughts about the lost will simply not exist, because such memories as they are will not exist. Instead, our memories will be reshaped and our minds taken up in the adoration of God, as we are absorbed in the great new works of his creative power; 'Be glad and rejoice *for ever* in what I will create.'—v. 18. According to the Book of Revelation the one who stands in the centre of the heavenly Jerusalem is Christ, the lamb who was slain, whose radiant presence will flood our hearts and minds with pure, liquid joy such that there won't be room for morbid thoughts.[10]

Far from boring

The new world is also a place where there is *freedom for service.*—v. 22b 'my chosen one's will enjoy the work of their hands, they will not toil in vain.'

If asked to describe their picture of heaven, the word many people would use would be 'boring'. George Bernard Shaw, in his typically pugnacious way, captured what most people think when he said: 'Heaven as conventionally conceived is a place so inane, so dull, so useless, so miserable that nobody would venture to describe a whole day in heaven, though plenty of people have described a day at the seaside.' Similarly, the writer, Laurie Lee declared: 'Heaven is too chaste, too disinfected, too much on its best behaviour. It receives little more than a dutiful nod from the faithful. Hell, on the other hand, is always a good crowd-raiser,

10. We read in Revelation 21, that there will be no 'mourning' (v4), so whatever the cause there will be no mourning of those who are lost.

having ninety percent of the action—high colours, high temperatures, intricate devilries, and always the most interesting company available.' The philosopher, A.J. Conyers also notes the disappearance of heaven from the popular mind, 'We live in a world no longer under heaven. At least in most people's minds and imaginations that vision of reality has become little more than a caricature, conjuring up the saints and angels of baroque frescoes. And in the church only a hint remains of the power it once exercised in the hearts of believers.'[11]

Shaw, strictly speaking, is correct, that is how heaven is *conventionally* conceived, as if all we will do all day is waft around on some cloud, clothed in a celestial negligee, strumming a golden harp. But that is not what the Bible pictures heaven being like any more than the new heaven and earth yet to come.

The Bible teaches that heaven will be a place of rest, but that is not the same as inactivity. Revelation 14:13 speaks of believers as being 'blessed, for they rest from their *labours.*' But the context makes it clear that the labour from which they are now released is that of spiritual warfare—battling against the world, the flesh and the devil. *Now* it is a battle, *then* it will be peace. Therefore, heaven is a rest not from work, but from woe.

While there will be rest in heaven there will also be activity

11. J. A. Conyers, *The Eclipse of Heaven: Rediscovering the Hope of a World Beyond* (Downers Grove, IL: InterVarsity Press, 1992), p. 11.

in heaven as hinted at here by these pictures, we shall 'labour' but unlike on earth there will be full satisfaction in what we do. The results won't disappoint us, either because we fail or someone else cuts in and reaps the benefits. Neither is work marred by pain or struggle. In Genesis 1 and 2 it is clear that we were created to work, to serve God as his vice regents.[12] In the new heaven and earth that purpose will be perfectly realised. There our human powers will be at full stretch, as renewed by grace and made perfect in love, they serve God in Christ.

The American theologian Jonathan Edwards put this prospect so beautifully: 'In heaven it is directly the reverse of what it is on earth; for there, by length of time things become more and more youthful, that is more vigorous, active, tender, more beautiful.' He concludes his sermon, *Heaven is a Place of Love* in this way:

And all of this in a garden of love, the Paradise of God, where everything has a cast of holy love, and everything conspires to promote and stir up love, and nothing to interrupt its exercises; where everything is fitted by an all-wise God for the enjoyment

---

12. 'The earth was given to man with this condition, that he should occupy himself in its cultivation … The custody of the garden was given in charge to Adam, to show that we possess the things that God has committed to our hands, on the condition, that being content with frugal and moderate use of them, we should take care of what shall remain … Let everyone regard himself as the steward of God in all things which he possesses. Then he will neither conduct himself dissolutely, nor corrupt by abuse those things which God requires to be preserved.' J. Calvin, *Commentary on Genesis*, J. King (trans, Banner of Truth, 1967) on Genesis 2:15.

of love under the greatest advantages. And all of this shall be without fading beauty of the objects beloved, or any decaying of love in the lover, and any satiety in the faculty which enjoys love. O! What tranquillity may we conclude there is such a world as this![13]

How this contrasts with the remarks of Shaw and Lee! Nothing can be more inspiring than Biblical thoughts of heaven.

Concluding remarks

We have called this book, *A Lost God in a Lost World* because in the West an awareness of the real God has been lost and replaced by idolatrous thoughts with the result that people are lost, that is, they become disorientated, dissatisfied and detached from God and so from reality. It is not coincidental that this 'loss of God' and 'loss of reality' has gone hand in hand with a loss in the belief of heaven and hell—the ultimate realities. There may not be a simple 'cause and effect' relationship between them, but there is undoubtedly *some* relationship. With God's transcendence diminished as he is 'located within', then invariably the focus of people's thinking and, in some cases, the church's ministry, will be focused on this world and everything will be prioritised accordingly. The 'otherworldliness' which characterised our forefathers in the faith with its long term view (Hebrews 11) is replaced by a this-worldliness and short term gain. Preaching is then developed which panders to this with its concern for 'how to' programmes. But as we have seen, those who have great

13. *The Works of Jonathan Edwards*, vol. 8, 385 (New Haven: Yale, 1992).

thoughts of God and great visions of the realities to come have been the most productive in this world. This needs to be regained if the church is to escape it present day captivity to 'Babylon'.

Strachan and Sweeney state well our present predicament and the much needed solution which has been the contention of this book:

> In a world stricken with a plague of narcissism and distractedness, it is essential that we recognise the truth about the afterlife now, while we may ready ourselves for the end. Death and the final judgement swiftly approach us all. In these last days, our only hope is to prepare ourselves for the end by seeking the one who holds eternity in His mighty hand.[14]

God's promise is clear and certain, 'Behold, *I will* create new heavens and a new earth' (Isaiah 65:17). May God's Church be both prepared and preparing in this day for that great day.

---

14. Owen Strachan and Doug Sweeney, *Jonathan Edwards on Heaven and Hell* (Moody Publications, 2010), p. 51.